D1740981

STRENGTHENING DOMESTIC RESOURCE MOBILIZATION IN SOUTHEAST ASIA

MAY 2022

ASIAN DEVELOPMENT BANK

Contents

Tables, Figures, and Box

Foreword

This publication is the second of four reports from a regional study completed in 2021 and funded by the technical assistance of the Asian Development Bank (ADB) on Policy Advice for COVID-19 Economic Recovery in Southeast Asia. The project supports the recovery efforts of Southeast Asian countries to return to their economic performance before the coronavirus disease (COVID-19) pandemic. It also assists countries in preparing for national, regional, or global transformations that may take place post-COVID-19. The focus countries are Cambodia, Indonesia, Myanmar, the Philippines, and Thailand, which tapped ADB's COVID-19 Pandemic Recovery Option facility.* The study produced four reports on the following thematic areas:

1. **Supporting post-COVID-19 economic recovery in Southeast Asia.** After analyzing different sectors, their potential for growth, and the strengths of economies in Southeast Asia, ADB identified five key sectors: tourism, agro-processing, and garments are well-established sectors needing transformation or improvement; while electronics and digital trade are evolving sectors with a high potential for growth. This allows the development of more targeted policies given the constraints to governments' financial and administrative resources.
2. **Strengthening domestic resource mobilization in Southeast Asia.** COVID-19 exacerbated the struggles of some governments to generate tax revenue to meet public expenditure needs. ADB proposes policy actions to expand the tax base, increase tax compliance, and strengthen tax administration to create a healthy fiscal space.
3. **Implementing a green recovery in Southeast Asia.** Green recovery from the pandemic is crucial to ensure an economically and environmentally resilient future for Southeast Asia. Well-designed policy measures can simultaneously achieve socioeconomic and environmental goals.
4. **Harnessing the potential of big data in post-pandemic Southeast Asia.** Digitalization gained more prominence amid COVID-19 and highlighted the value of big data for the effective and efficient delivery of key public services such as health care, social welfare and protection, and education. A range of policy enablers for big data adoption in policy making—from strategic governance to building a data driven culture—were examined.

This publication provides policy makers with a baseline to understand the scope of policy options available in their pursuit of economic recovery. There is still much uncertainty on timing, particularly as the trajectory of the pandemic (i.e., new COVID-19 mutations) remains unclear and countries await the development and distribution of more vaccines. While COVID-19's impact on Southeast Asia has been significant, the report provides hope. The medium-term growth opportunities are strong. Taking advantage of those opportunities, however, will require a significant rethink of current approaches. This series of publications will hopefully inspire governments to think beyond the containment stage and lay the groundwork for opportunities that will ensure a sustainable recovery underpinned by more resilient economies and societies.

The research benefited from the insights and perspectives of government officials, the private sector, the academe, and other key stakeholders and experts working in the region who convened in thematic workshops, roundtable consultations, and focus group discussions. We are grateful for their support and collaboration.

---

* ADB's stance on Myanmar since 1 February 2021 is outlined in its public statements of 2 February 2021 and 10 March 2021.

The ADB resident mission offices of the focus countries have effectively coordinated all country consultations to inform the study. We look forward to ADB's continued engagement with these countries, in line with its current approaches, to carry out the policy recommendations to support the region's recovery efforts. These recommendations align with the operational directions on fostering regional cooperation and integration under ADB's Strategy 2030. Strengthening regional cooperation is crucial for dealing with future crises more effectively.

Ramesh Subramaniam
Director General
Southeast Asia Department
Asian Development Bank

Acknowledgments

The research was supported by the regional technical assistance on Policy Advice for COVID-19 Economic Recovery in Southeast Asia (TA 9964). The team from the Regional Cooperation and Operations Coordination Division (SERC), Southeast Asia Department (SERD) of the Asian Development Bank (ADB) led by Thiam Hee Ng, former principal economist, SERC, with support from Dulce Zara and Georginia Nepomuceno managed the study and coordinated the preparation of this publication under the supervision of Alfredo Perdiguero, director, SERC. Jason Rush provided technical support. Maria Theresa Bugayong and Hannah Estipona extended administrative assistance.

The study is a collaboration between ADB and AlphaBeta (SG) PTE LTD led by Fraser Thompson. Stefano Scuratti from AlphaBeta prepared the report. Several ADB staff provided invaluable comments, including Jose Antonio Tan, Aekapol Chongvilaivan, Jhelum Thomas, Daisuke Miura, Go Nagata, David Freedman, and Chitchanok Annonjarn.

The team gratefully acknowledges the views and suggestions of government officials, the private sector, the academe, researchers, development partners, and other stakeholders in the region. They generously extended their support and cooperation during the thematic workshops, roundtable consultations, focus group discussions, and related events at the Southeast Asia Development Symposium 2021 conducted as part of the stakeholder engagement undertaken for this project. Special thanks to the ADB resident mission offices in Cambodia, Indonesia, Myanmar, the Philippines, and Thailand for coordinating the participation of in-country stakeholders in the workshops and consultation meetings as well as organizing meetings with fiscal authorities in respective countries. The report greatly benefited from consultation sessions with the Ministry of Economy and Finance, Cambodia; the Tax Compliance Affairs, Ministry of Finance, Indonesia; the Department of Finance of the Philippines; and the Revenue Department, Ministry of Finance, Thailand. Very thoughtful insights were also provided by PROSPERA (Australia Indonesia Partnership for Economic Development), Annette Chooi, Athiphat Muthitacharoen, Renato Reside, Jr., and Vid Adrison.

Effective 1 February 2021, ADB placed a temporary hold on sovereign project disbursements and new contracts in Myanmar. The bank continues to monitor the situation in the country. All of the background assessments in this study were undertaken before 1 February 2021.

The Knowledge Support Division of ADB's Department of Communications facilitated the publishing of this study.

Abbreviations

ADB	Asian Development Bank
BAU	business-as-usual
BEPS	base erosion and profit shifting
COVID-19	coronavirus disease
GDP	gross domestic product
IMF	International Monetary Fund
MSME	micro, small, and medium-sized enterprises
OECD	Organisation for Economic Co-operation and Development
PIT	personal income tax
TRAIN	Tax Reform for Acceleration and Inclusion
VAT	value-added tax

Executive Summary

With the success of the coronavirus disease (COVID-19) vaccine rollout in 2021 in Southeast Asia, governments are starting to shift their focus from immediate pandemic response toward economic recovery. As of December 2021, a total of close to $914 billion worth of COVID-19 response measures had been announced by Southeast Asian countries. This extraordinary fiscal expenditure has been mirrored by declines in the tax base, due to the combined effect of decreasing income and profit levels. Tax compliance has also suffered, and, while complete data for 2020 is not yet available, examples point to declines in individual and corporate tax filings in several countries. This points to significant risks to tax revenue levels, which are likely to remain subdued in the medium term. Optimal domestic resource mobilization (particularly tax collection and administration) will be a core enabler in the transition from emergency to recovery, as countries will need to balance fiscal sustainability concerns with the need to invest to support economic growth.

This report provides an assessment of domestic resource mobilization in five Southeast Asian countries: Cambodia, Indonesia, Myanmar, the Philippines, and Thailand. Global benchmarks point to a significant opportunity for these countries to improve tax collection. As of 2019, tax-to-gross domestic product (GDP) ratios averaged only 13.7%, with substantial variation and performance as low as 7% in Myanmar. The size of the prize that comes with optimizing domestic resource mobilization is large. If the five countries were to experience tax-to-GDP ratio increases by 2025 in line with top performers in the region, this could create about $216 billion in cumulative tax revenues above business-as-usual, almost double the combined GDP of Brunei Darussalam, Cambodia, and Myanmar.

Capturing this prize will require overcoming several challenges, many of which are long-standing and predate the pandemic. Some of the most significant in the focus countries include the following:
- The impact of subnational government revenues is limited. They account for only 4% of GDP on average (compared to 8.1% in the Asia Pacific region and over 15% in economies where fiscal decentralization is more advanced such as Australia and Japan).
- Tax progressivity is generally low, especially if compared to advanced economies. Among the focus countries, the Philippines and Thailand have the highest maximum tax rate of 35%, whereas Cambodia imposes only 20% as its highest rate. Similarly, the application of wealth taxes is limited to property tax and inheritance tax, both of which are underutilized.
- Informality is a major issue, with economy-wide estimates placing the size of the shadow economy up to 43% of GDP in Thailand and 33% in Cambodia, compared to less than 7% in Switzerland.
- International tax avoidance and evasion practices have emerged as key compliance risks, with Indonesia, the Philippines, and Thailand indicating base erosion and profit shifting as a high-risk area in the 2018 International Survey on Revenue Administration.
- Value-added tax (VAT) fraud is common and VAT efficiency ratios are low. For instance, Indonesia's VAT efficiency ratio of 0.36 lags behind regional leaders like Singapore (0.71) and is lower than all Organisation for Economic Co-operation and Development (OECD) countries.
- Tax administrations may suffer from institutionalized corruption, tax evasion, and tax revenue leakage. A comparative analysis conducted in 2015 points to relatively low tax administration staff strength in Cambodia, Indonesia, Myanmar, and the Philippines. Digitalization of the public administration is also a challenge.
- Tax compliance requires significant resources. The cost of paying taxes is generally high and according to a survey, over 80% of businesses find tax compliance and reporting obligations to be complicated.

Fortunately, there are large opportunities to improve tax collection and ease compliance. These opportunities can be grouped into three categories: (i) optimizing the tax structure, (ii) improving compliance, and (iii) simplifying the process of paying taxes. These three areas offer opportunities to build a bigger revenue pool through the introduction of new taxes (or the adjustment of existing ones) as well as by expanding the number of taxpayers, through an increase in the efficiency of the tax collection process by ensuring that taxpayers are compliant in domestic and international tax matters, and through simplification of the process of paying taxes. These opportunities are designed to target the key common challenges highlighted, but where short-to medium-term action is possible and does not require multilateral efforts. Within these three groups, governments can consider 10 specific opportunities:

- **Broadening personal income tax through increased tax progressivity.** Progressivity-focused reforms can generate some impact by increasing revenue from existing taxpayers, and significant medium-term impact if accompanied by measures to increase tax compliance and reduce the size of the informal economy. For example, an International Monetary Fund-proposed personal income tax reform package for Indonesia could raise an additional 0.3% of GDP by the end of the reform, including by revising the income under assessment from family income to personal income. A critical component of reforming progressivity is the revision of deductions and incentives, which tend to be complex (therefore disproportionally benefiting more sophisticated, high-earning taxpayers) and seldom reviewed.

- **Taxing wealth.** Wealth taxes present the advantage that they have an immediate impact and can be designed to target individual income groups to maximize revenue mobilization without depressing consumption. Inheritance tax is a form of wealth tax on intergenerational transfers. It is common in OECD economies, but limited in the focus countries, with only Thailand and the Philippines having measures in place. Administrative challenges, most notably disclosure and valuation, represent a key limitation to the potential impact of such measures, stressing the importance of a planning phase to maximize tax compliance as a precondition.

- **Taxing property.** Property taxation, if well designed, is regarded as one of the best forms of taxation for contributing to social equity because of its progressive nature. It is also advantageous because it is difficult to avoid, given the high visibility and immobility of land and buildings. Recent initiatives look to address common issues that governments in the region face, including poor system design, exemptions, incomplete property databases, and weak administration.

- **Taxing environmental externalities.** Despite significant environmental challenges and fiscal deficits in financing sustainable development, environmental tax regimes are limited. Conversely, fossil fuels consumption subsidies are common. Effective pricing of externalities presents a significant opportunity for governments to raise revenues while promoting a green transition, shifting the tax base from labor to resources.

- **Taxing digital services.** Estimates of the size of the digital economy range from 4.5% to 15.5% of world GDP. As the digital sector emerges as a key growth engine, identifying tax models that balance revenue collection and support of sector growth represents a significant opportunity. Tax administrations that are pursuing these initiatives are looking to strike a balance between achieving immediate results from a revenue mobilization perspective while advancing domestic policies that align with global tax initiatives. It will be critical to avoid jeopardizing growth of the digital economy and potentially inducing reciprocal action from overseas markets that could lose on their share of tax revenues.

- **Shrinking the informal economy.** Taxing the informal sector has been linked to accelerating growth of firms in the formal economy, sustaining tax morale, improving governance, and expanding the tax base. Besides limiting tax revenue, informality presents a challenge to effective tax expenditure and welfare, as unregistered individuals fail to benefit from social protection measures. Registering individuals and businesses as taxpayers (including linking access to services to a tax identity) is a critical first step, and an enabler to further measures to increase their tax compliance. At the corporate level, governments can mainstream tax registration, for example by linking it to business registration.

- **Tackling value-added tax fraud.** Opportunities to address this vary in terms of complexity. Data recording technologies, referred to as fiscal control units in some countries, help to secure sales data in point-of-sale systems so that tampering by phantomware can be prevented. The growth of the digital economy, and in particular online sales, offers opportunities to introduce e-invoicing methods, real-time VAT reporting, and blockchain applications.

- **Making online tax lodgment simple.** Well-designed tax portals can allow taxpayers to file their return, track their refunds, make online payments, obtain a copy of their prior year's return or income details to access other services, and be able to do all this through one single access account. Increasing the convenience to taxpayers through integrated services helps to improve tax compliance.

- **Easing the tax payment process.** Different forms of digital payments (i.e., internet banking, mobile payments, direct debit, etc.) can be used to increase the convenience for payers and lower the risk of late or nonpayment. Providing means for taxpayers (both individuals and corporates) to conveniently settle their obligations using internet banking portals is proven to lead to more timely receipts.

- **Enhancing communication with taxpayers.** Ensuring that tax administrations are accessible, transparent, and engaged presents short-term opportunities to support tax compliance and long-term opportunities to improve tax culture. Educational campaigns and use of social media have generated important results where effectively introduced.

Tax reform is complex and needs to account for several factors, including technical assessments as well as political economy considerations. A further important consideration is understanding the readiness of countries to implement certain tax reforms. For some countries, the focus should be on "basic readiness" measures that relate to foundational reforms needed. For other countries that are at an "advanced readiness" stage, the implementing measures can focus on more complex or additive interventions to fully capture the opportunity. Often, the ideal strategy will involve a mix of both basic and advanced measures, as countries can leverage areas where they have an existing advantage.

Ten opportunities to improve domestic resource mobilization in Southeast Asia could generate over $216 billion in tax revenue

Expanding the tax base
- Increasing PIT progressivity
- Taxing wealth
- Taxing property
- Environmental taxation
- Taxing digital services

Enhancing tax compliance
- Tackling informality
- Curbing VAT fraud

Enhancing tax administration
- Making tax lodgment simple
- Easing the payment process
- Enhancing tax communication

Challenges across three dimensions of domestic resource mobilization

Tax structure
- Limited role of sub-national taxation
- Low tax progressivity

Tax compliance
- High informality
- International tax avoidance
- Vulnerability to VAT fraud
- Low administrative capacity

Ease of compliance
- High administrative burden of tax compliance

Tax-to-GDP ratio increase in all Southeast Asian countries by 2025 in line with top performers in the region could create $216 billion in cumulative tax revenue above business-as-usual

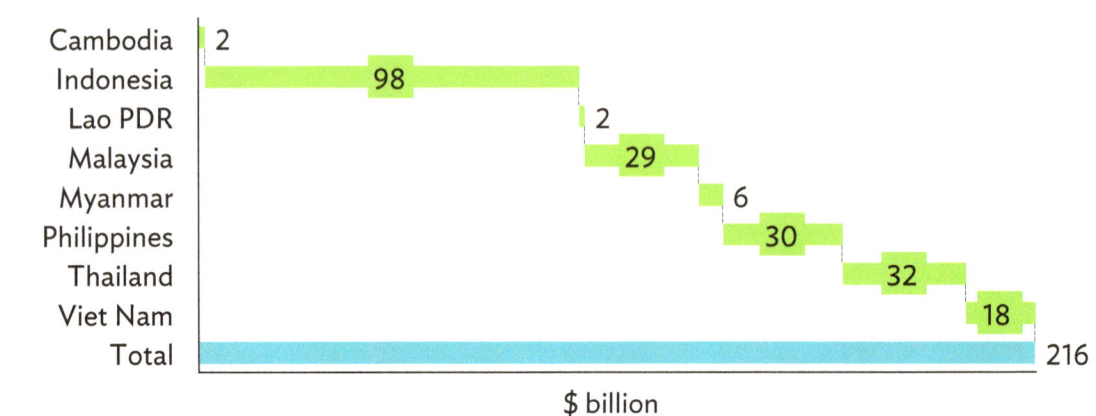

Country	$ billion
Cambodia	2
Indonesia	98
Lao PDR	2
Malaysia	29
Myanmar	6
Philippines	30
Thailand	32
Viet Nam	18
Total	216

$ billion

BAU = business as usual, GDP = gross domestic product, Lao PDR = Lao People's Democratic Republic, PIT = personal income tax, VAT = value-added tax.

Source: Authors.

SECTION I

Introduction

With the success of the coronavirus disease (COVID-19) vaccine rollout in 2021 in Southeast Asia, governments are starting to shift their focus from immediate response toward recovery. As of December 2021, close to a total of $914 billion worth of COVID-19 response measures had been announced by Southeast Asian economies, with Cambodia, Indonesia, Myanmar, the Philippines, and Thailand combined committing more than $527 billion. Unparalleled fiscal expenditure has been coupled by a substantial reduction in the tax base, partly because of subdued economic growth and partly because of underlying public finance management issues, which have been exacerbated by the pandemic. Optimal domestic resource mobilization (particularly tax collection and administration) will be a core enabler in the transition from emergency to recovery, as countries will need to balance fiscal sustainability concerns with the need to invest to support economic growth. This report shows that governments in the region can take immediate action to support their domestic resource mobilization initiatives through three sets of responses: (i) expanding the tax base, (ii) maximizing tax compliance, and (iii) simplifying tax compliance processes. Ten opportunities across these three areas can help governments in the focus countries strengthen their fiscal position.

▶ **Close to $914 billion has been committed by governments in Southeast Asia to date in tackling the COVID-19 pandemic, while tax revenues are falling.**

The five focus countries have suffered significant social and economic distress throughout the pandemic and measures to support the economy have taken a toll on public finances. According to the Asian Development Bank (ADB) COVID-19 Policy Database, a total of $914 billion worth of COVID-19 response measures were announced by Southeast Asian economies, with Cambodia, Indonesia, Myanmar, the Philippines, and Thailand combined committing more than $527 billion (Figure 1).[1]

Extraordinary expenditure has been mirrored by declines in the tax base. The focus countries are facing losses in tax revenue due to the combined effect of declining income and profit levels. Tax compliance has also suffered, and while full data are not yet available, anecdotal examples point to declines in individual and corporate tax filings. This points to significant risks to tax revenue levels, which are likely to remain subdued in the medium term (i.e., 1–3 years). Countries will need to adapt to various scenarios for the economic recovery in 2022 and beyond, with clear strategies to mitigate risks—global and local, and health and socio-economic. Some evidence from the focus countries is detailed below.

- **Cambodia.** Although overall tax revenue surpassed expectations for 2020 according to Cambodia's General Department of Taxation, forecasts for the 2021 Budget have been downgraded to below 2020 levels to account for the impact of the pandemic and associated economic slowdown.[2] Tax revenue in the first three quarters of 2021 was reported 3% lower than the level achieved in the same period in 2020. Growth forecast was revised down to around 2% in 2021 as the prolonged outbreak of COVID-19 was expected to disturb recovery in industry and services sectors.[3]

---

[1] ADB COVID-19 Policy Database. https://covid19policy.adb.org/ (accessed 31 December 2021).
[2] *The Phnom Penh Post.* 2020. General Department of Taxation's tax Collection Unfazed by Covid. https://www.phnompenhpost.com/business/gdts-tax-collection-unfazed-covid.
[3] ADB. 2021. *Asian Development Outlook 2021 Update. Transforming Agriculture in Asia.* https://www.adb.org/sites/default/files/publication/726556/ado2021-update.pdf.

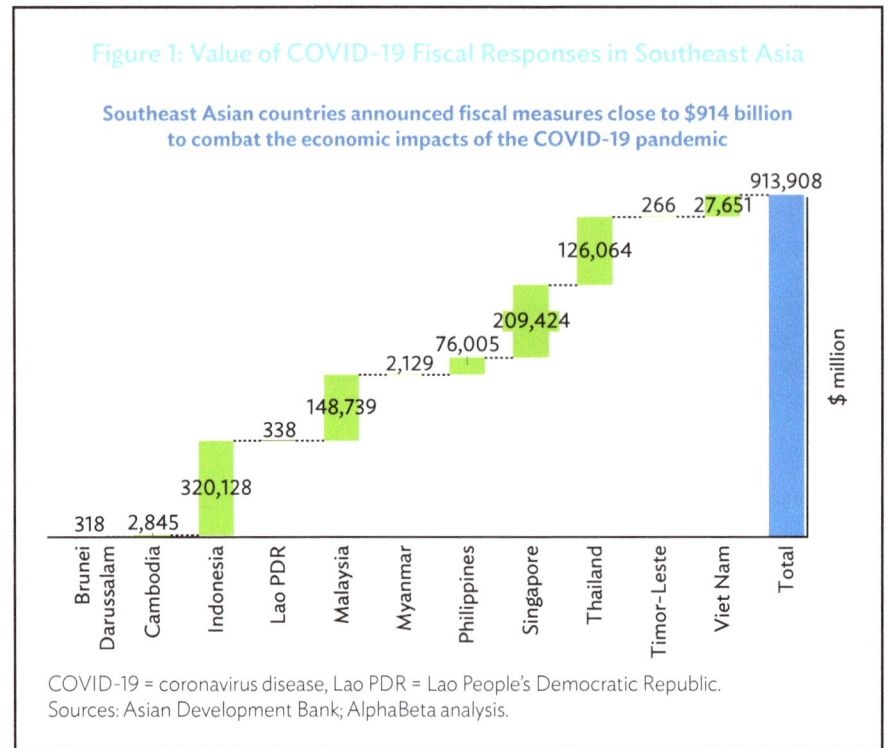

Figure 1: Value of COVID-19 Fiscal Responses in Southeast Asia

Southeast Asian countries announced fiscal measures close to $914 billion to combat the economic impacts of the COVID-19 pandemic

COVID-19 = coronavirus disease, Lao PDR = Lao People's Democratic Republic.
Sources: Asian Development Bank; AlphaBeta analysis.

- **Indonesia.** Annual individual filings in Indonesia decreased from 11.3 million to 9.4 million year-on-year in April 2020, whereas corporate filings declined from 452,027 to 412,166 over the same period.[4] In 2020, revenues were anticipated to be at least 20% below projections because of the slowdown in economic activity as well as the tax relief provided as part of COVID-19 economic response measures.[5] Fiscal policy was accommodative through 2021, with a deficit of 6.1% of gross domestic product (GDP) in 2020 (up from 2.2% in 2019), and about 4.5% in 2021.[6] Well-prioritized tax and expenditure reforms to improve the fiscal space, coupled with structural reforms to boost investment and productivity, will be important to achieve a stable recovery.

- **Myanmar.** Tax collections fell by 37% in FY2021 in comparison with the previous year.[7] Myanmar was hard hit by both second (mid-August 2020 to early January 2021) and third wave (mid-2021) of the pandemic. Moreover, the political crisis that started on 1 February 2021 has extensively destabilized the economy and halted an expected economic recovery from the COVID-19 pandemic. The economy contracted by 8.5% year-on-year in the second quarter of FY2021 (January-March), with the dual shocks stemmed from the pandemic and political tensions.[8] Economic growth is estimated to remain contracted in 2021, following significant economic disruptions across sectors. Growth outlook remained highly uncertain with ongoing political instability (footnote 3).

[4] A. Akhlas. 2020. Tax office keeps tax return deadline as filings plunge amid COVID-19. *The Jakarta Post.* 27 April. https://www.thejakartapost. com/news/2020/04/27/tax-office-keeps-tax-return-deadline-as-filings-plunge-amid-covid-19.html.

[5] ADB. 2020. *Indonesia 2020–2024—Emerging stronger.* https://www.adb.org/sites/default/files/institutional-document/640096/cps-ino-2020-2024.pdf.

[6] ADB. 2020. *Asian Development Outlook 2020 Update: Wellness in Worrying Times.* https://www.adb.org/sites/default/files/publication/635666/ado2020-update.pdf.

[7] Central Statistical Organization. 2021. *Selected Monthly Economic Indicators October 2021.* https://www.mopf.gov.mm/sites/default/files/upload_pdf/2021/12/SMEI%20(OCT21)_0.pdf.

[8] Central Bank of Myanmar. 2021. *Quarterly Financial Statistics Bulletin 2021 Volume I.* https://www.cbm.gov.mm/sites/default/files/report/2021/2021%20Vloume%20I.pdf.

- **Philippines.** Tax revenues rose by 9.6% year-on-year in the first 11 months of 2021, rebounding from the 11.4% decline in full-year 2020.[9] Economic recovery gained traction with GDP rising by 7.7% in the fourth quarter of 2021 to 5.6% for the full year, following a 9.6% decline in 2020. Private consumption and business activities bounced back as the economy gradually reopened. Imports rebounded in line with domestic demand. Public expenditure continued to rise, including spending on big infrastructure projects. The budget deficit rose by 24.6% year-on-year in the first 11 months of 2021. The budget deficit is programmed at 9.3% of GDP in 2021 from 7.6% of GDP in 2020. Government debt rose to 60.5% at the end of 2021 from 54.6% at the end of 2020 (footnote 9).

- **Thailand.** Tax revenue saw a 1.3% year-on-year expansion during the fiscal year 2020/2021 on the back of large imports expansion and improving domestic economic activities.[10] Overall collections fell below targets for the fiscal year by around 11.5%. Increased corporate vulnerabilities and high household debt risks remain—Thailand is second in the region on the latter figure at 89.3% of GDP as of September 2021.[11] Fiscal deficit widened as the government ramped up spending to shield households and businesses—rising by 4.8% of GDP for the year ending 2021—and public debt to GDP rising to 58.2% at the end of September 2021.[12] The economy is projected to rebound to 3.5–4.5% growth in 2022[13] but premature withdrawal of fiscal and financial relief could hinder the country's recovery.

---

[9] Philippine Bureau of Treasury. https://www.treasury.gov.ph.
[10] *Fiscal Policy Office.* 2021. https://www.fpo.go.th/main/getattachment/News/Press-conference/15014/196-2564-%E0%B9%81%E0%B8%96%E
0%B8%A5%E0%B8%87%E0%B8%82%E0%B9%88%E0%B8%B2%E0%B8%A7-%E0%B8%81%E0%B8%95-%E0%B8%A3%E0%B8%B2%E0-
%B8%A2%E0%B9%84%E0%B8%94%E0%B9%89-0964.pdf.aspx.
[11] Bank of Thailand. 2020. *Loans to Households.* https://www.bot.or.th/App/BTWS_STAT/statistics/BOTWEBSTAT.
aspx?reportID=775&language=eng.
[12] Public Debt Management Office. 2021. *Public Debt FY 1998 to the Present.* https://www.pdmo.go.th/en/public-debt/debt-outstanding.
[13] Office of the National Economic and Social Development Council. 2022. *Thai Economic Performance in Q4 of 2021 and the Outlook for 2022.t.*
https://www.bot.or.th/English/MonetaryPolicy/MonetPolicyComittee/MPR/Pages/default.aspx.

SECTION II

Challenges Facing Tax Regimes in Southeast Asia

▶ **Even before the COVID-19 pandemic, many Southeast Asian countries faced taxation challenges.**

A country's tax capacity, its ability to extract revenues to provide public goods, depends on several economic and demographic factors (including population size, resource endowment, industry sector composition, level of corruption, size of the informal economy, and quality of the bureaucracy). Tax structures (i.e., the mix of taxes used to generate revenue) are built on comparable pillars but their mix varies across countries. As a result, tax-to-GDP ratios differ substantially worldwide.[14] Southeast Asian countries are no different, with variation across revenue size, sources, impact of nonrevenue taxes (e.g., commodity sales and investment income), levels of decentralization in collection and administration, and overall institutional capacity of tax administrations. Nonetheless, global benchmarks point to a significant opportunity for many countries in the region to improve tax collection (Figure 2). Tax-to-GDP ratios average 13.7% in the focus countries, but with substantial variations in performance.[15]

▶ **A closer look at the five focus countries reveals some encouraging reforms.**

Focusing on Cambodia, Indonesia, Myanmar, the Philippines, and Thailand, there has been mixed progress in the countries' ability to raise their tax-to-GDP ratios over the past 5 years, with steady rates in Indonesia and Myanmar, improvements in Cambodia and the Philippines, and a slight decline in Thailand. While trends in tax-to-GDP ratios are susceptible to the impact of changes in economic growth, an assessment of existing challenges points to several commonalities as well as substantial opportunities through effective tax reform. Several initiatives are ongoing or have been completed, including:[16]

- Cambodia's Revenue Mobilization Strategy 2019–2023 (launched in 2019), focusing on automation of tax services, review of tax incentives, and the establishment of key performance indicators.
- Indonesia's Directorate General of Taxes completed a reform program, focusing on the introduction of risk-based audits, lifting bank secrecy, and development of information technology systems (focus areas that will form part of the medium-term revenue strategy include value-added tax [VAT], withholding tax, and a focus on wealthy Indonesians).
- Myanmar (as of January 2021) has developed reform goals to strengthen revenues. Internal Revenue Department is expanding the coverage of the self-assessment system and centralizing tax return and payment processing for the large and medium taxpayer offices. These are done to support reform goals including the broadening of the tax base while lowering rates, moving toward a greater reliance on indirect taxes, moving toward self-assessment in direct taxation, and improving the capacity of the tax administration.

[14] OECD. 2018. *Domestic Revenue Mobilisation: A New Database on Tax Levels and Structures in 80 Countries.* https://www.oecd.org/tax/tax-policy/domestic-revenue-mobilisation-a-new-database-on-tax-levels-and-structures-in-80-countries.pdf.
[15] ADB. 2020. Key Indicators Database. https://kidb.adb.org/kidb/ (accessed 30 December 2020).
[16] ADB. 2021. *A Comprehensive Assessment of Tax Capacity in Southeast Asia.* https://www.adb.org/sites/default/files/publication/751846/assessment-tax-capacity-southeast-asia.pdf.

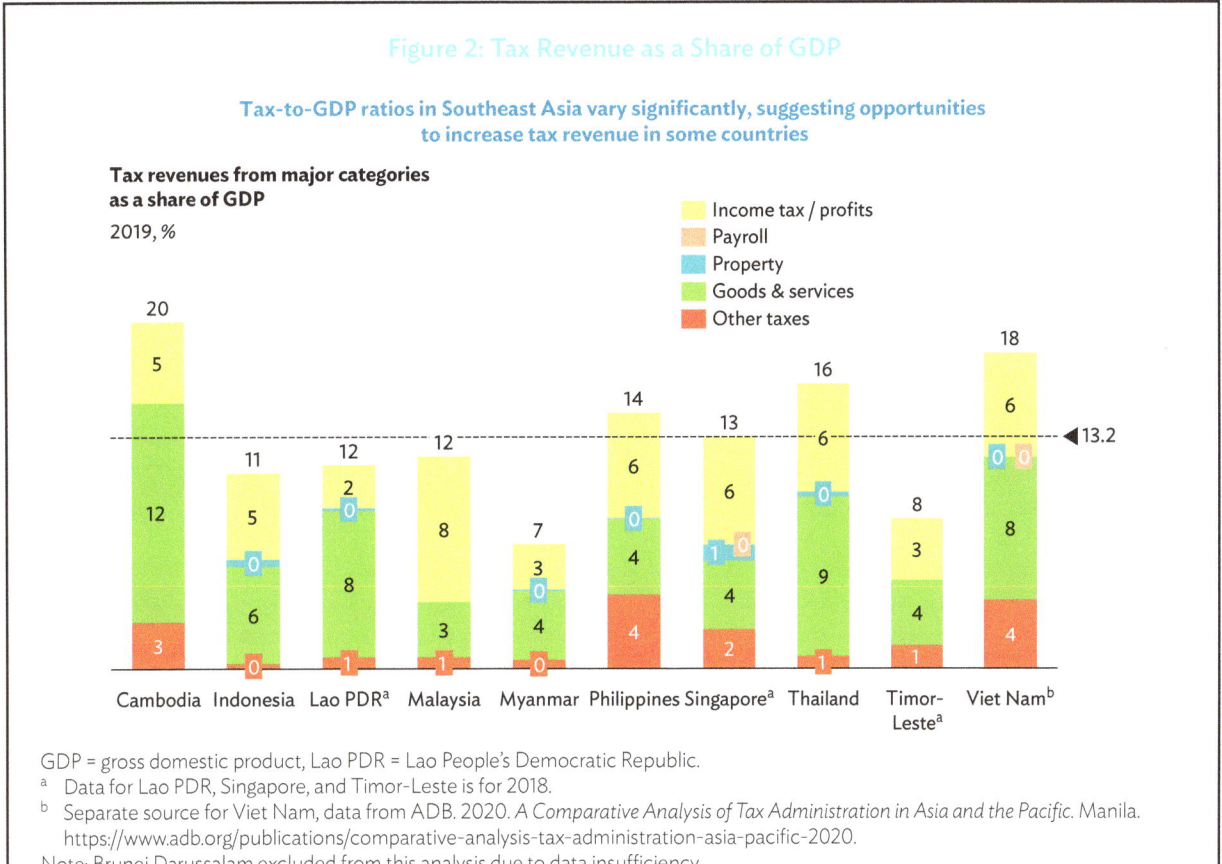

Figure 2: Tax Revenue as a Share of GDP

Tax-to-GDP ratios in Southeast Asia vary significantly, suggesting opportunities to increase tax revenue in some countries

Tax revenues from major categories as a share of GDP

2019, %

Legend:
- Income tax / profits
- Payroll
- Property
- Goods & services
- Other taxes

GDP = gross domestic product, Lao PDR = Lao People's Democratic Republic.

[a] Data for Lao PDR, Singapore, and Timor-Leste is for 2018.

[b] Separate source for Viet Nam, data from ADB. 2020. *A Comparative Analysis of Tax Administration in Asia and the Pacific.* Manila. https://www.adb.org/publications/comparative-analysis-tax-administration-asia-pacific-2020.

Note: Brunei Darussalam excluded from this analysis due to data insufficiency.

Sources: ADB; AlphaBeta analysis.

Box: Is there an Optimal Tax-to-GDP Ratio?

An important question when thinking about optimal taxation rates is around the impact of taxation on growth. In an influential paper, Gaspar et al. investigate whether there is a minimum tax-to-GDP ratio associated with a significant acceleration in the process of growth and development of an economy.[a] Using two large panel datasets, their study suggests that the answer is yes (i.e., that there is a minimum tax-to-GDP ratio needed to support accelerated economic growth), finding that countries' tipping points are similar, at about 12.75% of GDP. Analysis on one of the datasets suggests that a country just above the threshold will have GDP per capita 7.5% larger after 10 years. The same study points to a slightly negative slope in the relationship past 15% of GDP, which aligns with the standard recommendation to countries with low tax-to-GDP levels to aim for levels of at least 15%. Of course, tax-to-GDP ratios tend to be much higher in advanced economies, with the Organisation for Economic Co-operation and Development averaging approximately 34%. Tax-to-GDP is just one measure of domestic resource mobilization effectiveness. For example, Singapore's 13.1% is widely compensated by other revenue sources such as land leases. Similarly, resource-rich economies such as Brunei Darussalam rely more heavily on nontax revenues, such as commodity exports. A key shortcoming of this measure is that it does not directly measure revenue collection effectiveness: assuming suboptimal collection rates, countries have room to generate additional revenue through additional taxes, or, preferably, greater efficiency in tax collection. Once countries reach a basic threshold and satisfactory efficiency levels in tax collection, other considerations guide the choice of what taxation levels to pursue. The provision of social security, healthcare, education, and other citizen services ultimately depends on political economy and societal considerations.

[a] V. Gaspar et al. 2016. Tax Capacity and Growth: Is there a Tipping Point? *IMF Working Paper* 16/234. https://www.imf.org/external/pubs/ft/wp/2016/wp16234.pdf.

- The Philippines's Comprehensive Tax Reform Program, including Package 1 of the Tax Reform for Acceleration and Inclusion (TRAIN) Act in 2017 (TRAIN—which lowered and simplified personal income taxes, and expanded the VAT base); Package 2 (Corporate Recovery and Tax Incentives for Enterprises Act—including corporate income tax cuts, greater flexibility in the grant of incentives, and a longer sunset period for firms currently enjoying incentives); Package 3 (focusing on real property valuation); Package 4 (Passive Income and Financial Intermediary Taxation Act—on taxation of passive income), and additional packages including a tax amnesty and the introduction of sin and mining taxes.[17]
- Thailand's ongoing initiatives to address revenue leakage (including in taxation of the digital economy and introduction of a new e-payment law) and enforcement of the new Land and Property Tax Law.

▶ **The five focus countries face some common challenges in relation to taxation.**

These initiatives highlight different levels of maturity in the tax reform process of the five countries but also point to common challenges that policy makers are considering, as well as emerging issues. These challenges often cut across tax base maximization (and optimization), compliance, and operational efficiency. Critically, COVID-19 has magnified these gaps in several ways. For example, declines in tax compliance reflect taxpayers' reaction to economic hardship but also point to operational challenges in tax lodgment, made difficult by lockdowns. Another example is the increase in the use of digital platforms for business transactions, which has created additional compliance gaps particularly among micro, small, and medium-sized enterprises (MSMEs). Tax registration of MSMEs is generally low in the focus countries and while there is an opportunity to tax transactions through digital platforms, this often does not happen. Seven common challenges are identified (Table 1) based on a review of governments' policy priorities, the International Survey on Revenue Administration, recommendations from Article IV Consultations of the International Monetary Fund (IMF), insights from the 2020 Southeast Asia Symposium on Domestic Resource Mobilization for COVID-19 Economic Recovery, and an assessment of structural issues.

A. Role of Subnational Taxation

Despite rising rates of urbanization and limited allocation of central funds to local development, fiscal decentralization is low in the five focus countries. With the exception of Indonesia, which has almost 84,000 subnational administrations across three levels of government, subnational government revenues account for only 4% of GDP on average (compared to 8.1% in the Asia Pacific region and over 15% in economies where fiscal decentralization is more advanced such as Australia and Japan). Subnational government expenditure is generally also limited, averaging 3.5% of GDP.[18] Low local tax revenues and weak expenditure efficiency represent a missed opportunity. For example, property-based taxation, a key source of subnational tax revenue for local administrations globally, is significantly underutilized. Property tax accounts for only 0.3% of GDP in the five focus countries, compared to an OECD average of 1.9%.[19] Property taxation is equivalent to 0.6% of GDP in Cambodia, 0.5% in Thailand, and 0.5% in the Philippines. By comparison, the Republic of Korea, one of the better performing countries in Asia and the Pacific, achieves a 3.1% ratio, whereas the highest performing countries in the world (France and the United Kingdom) achieve a 4% ratio.[20] Fiscal decentralization processes

---

[17] Philippines Comprehensive Tax Reform Program. https://taxreform.dof.gov.ph/.

[18] UCLG. 2020. *The Localization of the Global Agendas. How Local Action is Transforming Territories and Communities.* https://www.gold.uclg.org/sites/default/files/ENG-ASPAC%20REGION%E2%80%94web-final.pdf.

[19] ADB. 2020. *A Comparative Analysis of Tax Administration in Asia and the Pacific.* Manila. https://www.adb.org/sites/default/files/publication/569626/tax-administration-asia-pacific-2020.pdf.

[20] ADB. 2020. *Mapping Property Tax Reform in Southeast Asia.* https://www.adb.org/sites/default/files/publication/666901/mapping-property-tax-reform-southeast-asia.pdf.

Table 1: Challenges to Taxation in the Focus Countries

Similar challenges to taxation across seven dimensions in focus countries

Improvement opportunity by country: ⬤ Large   ⬤ Some   ⬤ Limited

	Challenge	Country				
		Cambodia	Indonesia	Myanmar	Philippines	Thailand
Tax structure	Role of subnational taxation[a]	Large	Some	Large	Large	Large
	Tax progressivity[b]	Large	Large	Large	Some	Some
Tax compliance	Informality[c]	Large	Large	Large	Some	Some
	International tax avoidance and taxation of cross-border services[d]	Some	Large	Some	Large	Large
	Vulnerability to VAT fraud[e]	Large	Large	Large	Large	Large
	Administrative capacity[f]	Some	Some	Some	Some	Limited
Ease of tax	Administrative burden of tax compliance[g]	Large	Some	Large	Some	Some

VAT = value-added tax.
a   Indexed based on subnational governments' tax revenue as a share of total revenue. (Limited: ≥10%; some: 10%> x >4%; large ≤4%).
b   Based on benchmarking of top tax rate relative to global averages. (Limited: >35%; some: 35%≥ x >25%; large ≤25%).
c   Share of informal workers based on total workers. (Limited: <30%; some: 30%≥ x >60%; large ≥60%).
d   Based on ISORA survey results and stakeholder interviews (Large: indicates as a high-risk area).
e   Assessed based on VAT efficiency ratios and stakeholder interviews.
f   Based on ADB. 2020. *A Comparative Analysis of Tax Administration in Asia and the Pacific.* Manila.
g   Index of three indicators of the World Bank's Paying Taxes survey (frequency of payments, hours to comply, post-filing challenges: see Table 2. Limited: at least 2/3 indicators score as limited; some: not more than 1 score as large; large: at least 2/3 indicators score as large).
Sources: Asian Development Bank, International Labour Organization, Organisation for Economic Co-operation and Development, United Cities and Local Governments, World Bank, various sources; AlphaBeta analysis.

are underway but common challenges range from effective implementation of legal frameworks to political instability, accountability of local administrations, and competition across different levels of government.

B.   Tax Progressivity

Equity considerations in tax policy are set to remain critical as countries transition from crisis response to recovery. Tax progressivity, one key indicator of the equity of the tax system, is limited. All focus countries impose a 0% minimum personal income tax (PIT) rate that exempts low earners. The Philippines and Thailand have the highest maximum tax rate of 35%, whereas Cambodia imposes only 20% as its highest rate.[21] These rates are comparatively low relative to advanced economies, where the top bracket of PIT can exceed 55%, for example, in France and Japan. The application of wealth taxes is also limited to property tax and inheritance tax, which are underutilized. Cambodia, Indonesia, and Myanmar have no meaningful inheritance taxes, while Thailand applies

---

21   ASEAN Briefing. 2018. *Comparing Tax Rates across ASEAN.* https://www.aseanbriefing.com/news/comparing-tax-rates-across-asean/.

a rate of up to 10% on amounts exceeding B100 million ($3.3 million) once outstanding debts are paid,[22] and the Philippines applies a 5% to 20% rate on the net estate of both residents and nonresidents.[23]

C. High Levels of Informality

Informality is a major issue across all five focus countries.[24] The International Labour Organization (ILO) estimates that as many as 93% of those who are employed in Cambodia are part of the informal economy, while the share in Myanmar and Indonesia is as high as 85%.[25] Other estimates point to shares in excess of 55% in Thailand[26] and 56% in the Philippines (the average annual rate over 2008–2017).[27] In comparison, the informal economy represents only 18% of Japan's total employment (footnote 25). The vast majority of these workers are either self-employed or employed in SMEs,[28] which represent the backbone of the economies of the focus countries. Most of them are employed in the agriculture sector, with the ratio of informal workers in rural areas exceeding 95% in Cambodia. This is a challenge, as high shares of agriculture in GDP are generally associated with lower tax-to-GDP ratios, as most people employed in the sector are on low incomes and are not registered for tax purposes.[29] Economy-wide estimates place the size of the shadow economy up to 43% of GDP in Thailand and 33% in Cambodia, compared to less than 7% in Switzerland.[30] A related challenge is around tax registrations, which are generally low. For example, only 19% of the working age population is registered for tax purposes in Indonesia (although often married couples file taxes using the same tax registration number, which might skew the figure).[31] This results in foregone tax on both personal and corporate income.

D. International Tax Avoidance and Taxation of Cross-Border Services

Globalization and growth in the digital economy have resulted in an increase in cross-border activity for the focus countries. International tax avoidance and evasion practices have emerged as key compliance risks, with Indonesia, the Philippines, and Thailand indicating base erosion and profit shifting (BEPS) as a high-risk area in the 2018 International Survey on Revenue Administration. BEPS refers to a set of tax avoidance measures that

---

[22] Note: Two rates are applied (5% and 10%). If the person receiving an inheritance is an ascendant or a descendant, the person shall pay tax at the rate of 5%. if not, the person shall pay at 10%.

[23] Deloitte. 2017b. *Shifting Sands: Risk and Reform in Uncertain Times, 2017 Asia Pacific Tax Complexity Survey.* https://www2.deloitte.com/lk/en/pages/tax/articles/asia-pacific-tax-complexity-survey.html.

[24] In contrast to the concept of the informal sector that refers to production units as observation units, the concept of informal employment refers to jobs as observation units.

[25] ILO. 2018. *Women and Men in the Informal Economy: A Statistical Picture.* https://www.ilo.org/wcmsp5/groups/public/---dgreports/---dcomm/documents/publication/wcms_626831.pdf.

[26] A. Buddhari and P. Rugpenthum. 2019. *A Better Understanding of Thailand's Informal Sector.* https://www.bot.or.th/Thai/MonetaryPolicy/ArticleAndResearch/FAQ/FAQ_156.pdf.

[27] M. Gonzales. 2019. *Size of the Informal Economy in the Philippines (presentation).* https://www.ilo.org/manila/eventsandmeetings/WCMS_634914/lang--en/index.htm.

[28] ILO. 2019. *Small Matters: Global Evidence on the Contribution to Employment by the Self-Employed, Micro-Enterprises and SMEs.* https://www.ilo.org/wcmsp5/groups/public/---dgreports/---dcomm/---publ/documents/publication/wcms_723282.pdf.

[29] P. Gupta. 2015. https://read.oecd-ilibrary.org/taxation/revenue-statistics-in-asian-countries-2017_9789264278943-en#page21.

[30] L. Medina and F. Schneider. 2018. *Shadow Economies Around the World: What Did We Learn Over the Last 20 Years?* https://www.imf.org/en/Publications/WP/Issues/2018/01/25/Shadow-Economies-Around-the-World-What-Did-We-Learn-Over-the-Last-20-Years-45583.

[31] OECD. 2019. *Raising More Public Revenue in Indonesia in a Growth- And Equity-Friendly Way.* http://www.oecd.org/officialdocuments/publicdisplaydocumentpdf/?cote=ECO/WKP(2019)3&docLanguage=En.

artificially displace profits on economic activities to lower-tax locations where such activities are limited or absent, curbing tax authorities' ability to collect revenues from domestic activities. Globally, BEPS practices cost countries $100 billion–$240 billion in lost revenue annually, which is equivalent to 4%–10% of the global corporate income tax revenue.[32] This has created a significant gap in countries' ability to effectively capture revenue from the transaction of cross-border services. This extends to transactions enabled by the digital economy.

E.   Vulnerability to Value-Added Tax Fraud

VAT fraud covers a range of illegal activities that result in loss of tax revenue that should have been remitted to authorities, usually through businesses under-reporting or misrepresenting their sales, and/or unlawful VAT recovery claims from tax authorities.[33] It includes businesses' failure to register with tax authorities, underreporting of business, income, inflation of costs, and claiming refunds or deductions for VAT that has not been paid by the supplier.[34] VAT fraud is a critical issue in the five focus countries, as revealed by relatively low VAT efficiency ratios in comparison with both regional peers and more advanced economies.[35] For instance, Indonesia's VAT efficiency ratio of 0.36 lags behind regional leaders like Singapore (0.71) and is lower than all OECD countries, ranging from Spain at the bottom (0.44) and Canada at the top (1.51).[36] Thailand (0.48) similarly lags behind regional and global leaders in VAT efficiency. The large shadow economy is an indicator of inefficiencies in VAT administration and reporting. VAT thresholds have been shown to play a role in determining compliance behaviors. For example, analysis on the distribution of Thai firms around VAT registration thresholds shows that the number of firms that report revenue above the threshold is significantly lower than expected, suggesting that firms respond strategically to thresholds adjusting their compliance behaviors.[37]

F.   Administrative Capacity

Institutional capacity is a key predictor of a country's ability to effectively mobilize domestic resources. Tax administrations may suffer from institutionalized corruption, tax evasion, and tax revenue leakage (footnote 14). A comparative analysis conducted in 2015 points to relatively low tax administration staff strength in Cambodia, Indonesia, Myanmar, and the Philippines (although revenue bodies in Cambodia and Indonesia received significant injections of additional staff since). The same analysis points to an exceedingly high share of staff dedicated to verification of tax returns in the Philippines (60% relative to an OECD average of 17%), potentially indicating a lag in digitalization.[38] To combat corruption and conflict of interest, national governments

---

[32] OECD. 2020. *OECD/G20 Inclusive Framework on BEPS.* http://www.oecd.org/tax/beps/flyer-inclusive-framework-on-beps.pdf.

[33] M. Walpole. 2014. *Tackling VAT Fraud. International VAT Monitor September/October 2014.* https://www.ibfd.org/sites/ibfd.org/files/content/pdf/ivm_2014_05_int_1.pdf.

[34] OECD. 2017. *Shining Light on the Shadow Economy.* https://www.oecd.org/tax/crime/shining-light-on-the-shadow-economy-opportunities-and-threats.pdf.

[35] VAT efficiency ratio (E) is defined as the share of the VAT in GDP divided by the standard VAT rate. An efficiency ratio of, say, 30%, implies that if the standard VAT rate is increased by one percentage point, the shares of the VAT revenues in GDP is expected to increase by 0.3 percentage point. Economically, this efficiency ratio reflects the ability of government to collect tax revenue. The lower it is, the higher is the difference between real and declared income, and the fewer economic agents pay taxes.

[36] OECD statistics, as quoted in: W. Winardi. 2016. Improving VAT Administration: Indonesia's Experience, Challenges and Solutions. IMF Seventh High Level Tax Conference for Asian Countries. Tokyo. https://www.imf.org/external/np/seminars/eng/2016/asiatax/pdf/ww6.pdf.

[37] A. Muthitacharoen et al. 2021. Tax Incentives to Appear Small: Evidence from Thai Firms and Corporate Groups. *PIER Discussion Papers* 148. Puey Ungphakorn Institute for Economic Research. Revised Feb 2021. https://ideas.repec.org/p/pui/dpaper/148.html.

[38] ADB. 2018. *A Comparative Analysis of Tax Administration in Asia and the Pacific: 2018 Edition.* https://www.adb.org/sites/default/files/publication/441166/tax-administration-asia-pacific-2018.pdf.

in many economies have established what are described as semiautonomous revenue authorities. This form of institutional setup is seen widely in both Africa and South America, although it is relatively rare in Asia (apart from Singapore's Inland Revenue Authority and Malaysia's Inland Revenue Board) and absent in the core countries. Semiautonomous revenue authorities are generally established to provide more autonomy in human resource and budget management matters, and to provide a level of insulation from political interference (footnote 38).

G.   High Administrative Burden of Tax Compliance

Designing a tax compliance system that will not discourage taxpayers from participating is critical to effective domestic resource mobilization. Firm survey data for 147 economies show that companies consider tax rates to be among the top five constraints to their operations and tax administration to be among the top 11.[39] According to an analysis from PricewaterhouseCoopers and the World Bank, the cost of paying taxes is generally high in the five focus countries (Table 2).[40] Frequency of payments (the total number of payments made with respect to taxes and mandatory contributions) is above the global average for Cambodia, Indonesia, and Myanmar. The amount of time businesses spend to comply is in line with global averages, although nearly 10 times as high as

Table 2: Ease of Tax Payment in the Five Focus Countries

Opportunities to improve the ease of tax payments in focus countries

Improvement opportunity by country: Large Some Limited

Ease of Tax Payment	Country					Global Average	Global Best Practice
	Cambodia	Indonesia	Myanmar	Philippines	Thailand		
Frequency of payments (# payments per year)[a]	40	26	31	13	21	23.1	3 (Hong Kong, China; and Bahrain)
Complexity of tax calculation (hours to comply)[b]	173	191	282	171	229	234	22.5 (Bahrain)
Post-filing challenges (index where 100 equals best performance)[c]	26	68.8	45.5	50	73.4	60.9	100 (Turkey)

[a]   Number of annual payments required for profit, labor and other taxes.
[b]   Total time per year for completing corporate, income and consumption taxes per person.
[c]   Examines the processes of correcting a corporate income tax return and claiming a value-added tax refund.
Source: PricewaterhouseCoopers and the World Bank. 2020. *Paying Taxes*. https://www.pwc.com/gx/en/paying-taxes/pdf/pwc-paying-taxes-2020.pdf.

[39]   World Bank. 2020. *World Bank Enterprise Surveys*. http://www.enterprisesurveys.org.
[40]   PricewaterhouseCoopers (PWC) and World Bank. 2020. *Paying Taxes 2020*. https://www.pwc.com/gx/en/services/tax/publications/paying-taxes-2020/overall-ranking-and-data-tables.html.

global best practice levels. Post filing (processes of correcting a corporate income tax return and claiming a VAT refund) presents challenges in Cambodia, Myanmar, and the Philippines. Performance across both frequency of payments and time to comply metrics has improved in Indonesia and the Philippines, whereas the other countries have mostly stagnated or worsened (footnote 40). This assessment broadly aligns with a 2017 Deloitte survey assessing taxpayers' perception of tax complexity. According to the survey, over 80% of respondents found tax compliance and reporting obligations in the focus countries (Cambodia was not included) to be complicated, with the share of respondents indicating so reaching up to 90% in Indonesia (footnote 23).

▶ **If all Southeast Asian countries experience tax-to-GDP ratio increases by 2025 in line with top performers in the region, this could create over $216 billion in cumulative tax revenues above a business-as-usual scenario.**

An IMF study provided an approach to look into the effects of tax changes during fiscal consolidations.[41] To understand the potential size of the prize from addressing these challenges and improving tax collection, the cumulative additional taxes that Southeast Asian economies could collect if they could improve their respective tax-to-GDP ratios to the level of top performers in the region was sized (Figure 3). To produce this estimate, an assessment was done on how tax-to-GDP ratios have evolved in the region in the last decade and the most significant improvers over a 5-year period were identified. To account for different starting points, different growth rates to countries above and below the 15% tax-to-GDP threshold were applied. Specifically, a higher potential (2.4% growth in tax-to-GDP ratios over 5 years) was found for countries starting from a lower (rate, and a more moderate potential (1.4%) for countries already above the 15% benchmark. Excluding Singapore and Brunei Darussalam, which are high income countries, and Timor-Leste, due to data volatility, there is a large potential increase in other countries in Southeast Asia. In fact, by moving in a linear fashion from current tax-to-GDP ratios to match the increases in the ratios of these top regional performers, these countries could capture an additional $216 billion in cumulative tax revenues (which is almost double the combined GDP of Brunei Darussalam, Cambodia, and Myanmar).[42]

[41] IMF. 2018. *Macroeconomic Effects of Tax Rate and Base Changes: Evidence from Fiscal Consolidations.* https://www.imf.org/~/media/Files/Publications/WP/2018/wp18220.ashx.
[42] For a full explanation of the approach, see Appendix A1.

Figure 3: Potential Additional Tax Revenues in Southeast Asia, 2021–2025

Tax-to-GDP ratio increase in all Southeast Asian countries by 2025 in line with top performers in the region could create $216 billion in cumulative tax revenue above business-as-usual

Potential increase in cumulative tax revenues vs. BAU projections[a,b]
2020–2025

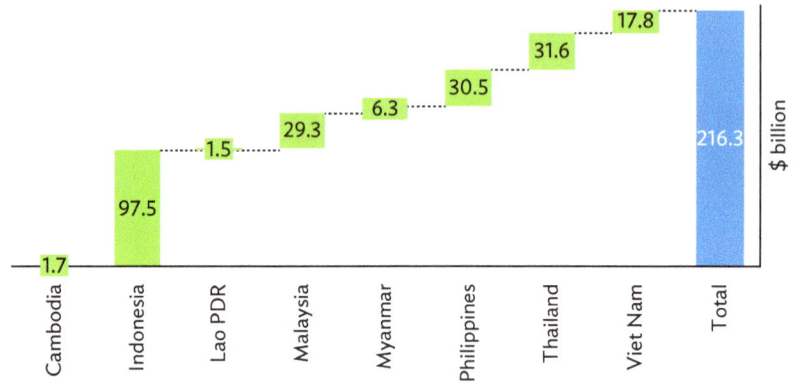

BAU = business-as-usual, Lao PDR = Lao People's Democratic Republic.

[a] BAU projections over 2020–2025 for tax-to-gross domestic product (GDP) ratio assumed to be the same as in the latest year of available data.

[b] Tax-to-GDP ratios vary significantly for economies with different underlying market characteristics, stages of economic development, and tax regimes, e.g. countries with socialist systems and welfare states have higher tax-to-GDP ratios; capitalist economies have lower tax collection relative to GDP; developed economies show little variation in their ratios (with some even declining as their tax rates remain stable while GDP rises). Accordingly, we split countries into two groups for this analysis—those with tax-to-GDP ratios above and below 15% in the latest year of available data, 15% being the rough threshold for countries with different underlying market characteristics. For ADB member countries with the top 10 ratios in each category, we assessed the growth rates in tax-to-GDP ratios of the top performing countries over the past 5 years of available data. Those with a ratio greater than 15% grew on average by 1.8% over the 5-year period, while those with ratios below 15% grew on average 2.44% over the 5-year period. These growth rates were then applied to the countries of the Association of Southeast Asian Nations considered in this analysis for the forecast period of 2020–2025, with tax-to-GDP ratios similarly considered above and below 15% and unique average growth rates of top performing ADB member countries in each category applied. This increase was distributed annually in a linear fashion from 2020–2025.

Note: This analysis excludes Brunei Darussalam and Singapore as they have graduated from regular ADB assistance. It also excludes Timor-Leste because of tax revenue data volatility, which makes it challenging to forecast future tax revenues.

Sources: World Bank; AlphaBeta analysis.

Policies to Strengthen Domestic Resource Mobilization

▶ **Ten opportunities in three areas could help enhance tax collection and ease compliance in the focus countries.**

Irrespective of countries' tax-to-GDP ratios, there are large opportunities to improve tax collection and ease compliance. These opportunities can be grouped into three categories: (i) optimizing the tax structure, (ii) improving compliance, and (iii) simplifying the process of paying taxes. These three areas offer opportunities to build a bigger revenue pool through the introduction of new taxes (or the adjustment of existing ones) as well as by expanding the number of taxpayers, through an increase in the efficiency of the tax collection process by ensuring that taxpayers are compliant in domestic and international tax matters, and through simplification of the process of paying taxes. The opportunities or areas of growth address the common challenges in taxation among the focus countries. The scope of the study is short to medium term. Table 3 shows opportunities for enhancing taxation in the five focus countries.

Table 3: Opportunities for Enhancing Taxation in the Focus Countries

Ten opportunities to expand the tax base, enhance compliance, and improve tax administration

Improvement opportunity by country:　■ Large　■ Some　■ Limited

	Opportunity	Country				
		Cambodia	Indonesia	Myanmar	Philippines	Thailand
Expanding the base	Increasing PIT progressivity	Large	Large	Large	Limited	Some
	Taxing wealth	Large	Large	Large	Some	Some
	Taxing property	Large	Large	Large	Some	Large
	Environmental taxation	Large	Large	Large	Large	Large
	Taxing digital services	Limited	Large	Limited	Large	Large
Enhancing compliance	Tackling informality	Large	Large	Large	Large	Some
	Curbing VAT fraud	Large	Large	Large	Some	Large
Improving tax administration	Marking tax lodgment simple	Large	Large	Large	Large	Some
	Easing the payment process	Large	Large	Large	Large	Some
	Enhancing tax communication	Large	Some	Large	Some	Some

PIT = personal income tax, VAT = value-added tax.
Source: AlphaBeta analysis.

Some of the policy measures discussed in this report can be actioned quickly and produce returns in a short timeframe; others are part of ongoing processes that will take longer to come to fruition but that can be accelerated as countries design fiscal consolidation strategies in the aftermath of the COVID-19 crisis.

A.   Expanding the Tax Base

Reliance on direct taxation is limited in the five core countries. Indonesia currently obtains 42% of its tax revenues from indirect taxes on goods and services,[43] the Philippines 43%,[44] and Thailand 57%.[45] This is a high rate if compared to OECD countries, where only 32% of tax revenues are from indirect taxes on average.[46] Some of this is due to tax design considerations (e.g., the relevance of commodity exports) and some to low levels of tax registration among businesses and individuals. Various tax measures can be considered to expand the countries' tax base. Effective introduction of these measures will require governments to identify the right balance between considerations on social equity, economic activity, and tax revenue maximization.[47] Some of the measures that are discussed in this report include introducing entirely new taxes. However, initiatives that seek to review the contribution of existing taxes are equally important. For example, rationalizing corporate income tax incentives can have a substantial impact. For example, tax holidays have been shown to present a differential of up to 12.4% between headline corporate income tax and effective tax rate under maximum incentives in Thailand.[48] Tools such as annual tax expenditure reports can offer an important resource to inform the current impact of tax exemptions on overall tax revenue levels, as well as a measure to gauge the exposure of proposed fiscal measures.[49]

1.   Broadening Personal Income Tax through Increased Tax Progressivity

Tax progressivity is widely accepted as a desirable approach to domestic resource mobilization due to its efficiency in maximizing contributions and social equity, showing a positive impact on societies' Gini coefficient.[50] Research shows that declining progressivity of PIT, especially at the upper end of the distribution, has contributed to reducing overall income redistribution in some countries.[51] Identifying the appropriate tax brackets and taxation levels is complex and dependent on a variety of other factors, including the contingent effect of indirect taxes. Nonetheless, current tax structures in the focus countries point to a set of opportunities, particularly where the progressivity of PIT is limited. This is the case in all five focus countries, where top rates are comparatively low. Some countries have begun reform in this direction. For example, the Philippines, through the introduction of the TRAIN 1 Package, excluded taxpayers with annual taxable income below PHP 250,000 and introduced lower tax rates ranging from 15% to 30% for most of the population, and an increase in tax from 32%

---

[43]   OECD. 2020. *Details of Public Revenue—Indonesia.* https://stats.oecd.org/Index.aspx?DataSetCode=REVIDN#.

[44]   OECD. 2020. *Details of Public Revenue—Philippines.* https://stats.oecd.org/Index.aspx?DataSetCode=REVIDN#.

[45]   OECD. 2020. *Details of Public Revenue—Thailand.* https://stats.oecd.org/Index.aspx?DataSetCode=REVIDN#.

[46]   OECD. 2019. *Revenue Statistics 2019: Tax Revenue Trends in the OECD.* https://www.oecd.org/tax/tax-policy/revenue-statistics-highlights-brochure.pdf.

[47]   A. Fieldhouse. 2013. *A Review of the Economic Research on the Effects of Raising Ordinary Income Tax Rates.* https://www.epi.org/publication/raising-income-taxes/.

[48]   A. Muthitacharoen. 2018. *Location Choice and Tax Responsiveness of Foreign Multinationals: Evidence from ASEAN Countries.* https://www.pier.or.th/files/dp/pier_dp_095.pdf.

[49]   Implementation of similar instruments requires a review of policies that grant tax preferences and determining a government's fiscal exposure arising from such laws. The drafting of a Tax Expenditure Report enabled the Philippine government to present quantitative evidence that certain past laws passed by Congress led to substantial fiscal exposure, which helped identify gaps and loopholes.

[50]   ESCAP. 2017. *Prospects for Progressive Tax Reform in Asia and the Pacific.* https://www.unescap.org/sites/default/files/S2_Prospects_for_Progressive_Tax_Reform.pdf.

[51]   E. Rubolino and D. Waldenstroem. 2017. *Tax Progressivity and Top Incomes: Evidence from Tax Reforms.* http://ftp.iza.org/dp10666.pdf.

to 35% for individual taxpayers whose annual taxable income exceeds ₱8 million ($166,000).[52] Tax exemptions and tax evasion are set to limit the short-term potential for such revenue.[53] However, these reforms can generate some impact by increasing revenue from existing taxpayers, and significant medium-term impact if accompanied by measures to increase tax compliance and reduce the size of the informal economy. For example, an IMF-proposed PIT reform package for Indonesia could raise an additional 0.3% of GDP by the end of the reform, including by revising the income under assessment from family income to personal income holding the basic exception constant, and revising the income bracket subject to the highest rate of 30%.[54] Advanced economies like Canada, Czech Republic, and Sweden saw significant increase in female labor force participation when using individual instead of family income taxation.[55] A critical component of reforming progressivity is the availability and nature of deductions and incentives. Consultations point to the fact that they tend to be complex (therefore disproportionally benefitting more sophisticated, high-earning taxpayers) and that they are not regularly reviewed. Tax expenditure reporting, which aims to assess the impact of preferential taxation, can offer a clear metric to assess the return on investment of tax exemptions and incentives. Another important consideration is around tax rate equitability and tax compliance behavior. Both are important elements in determining the optimal shape of a country's Laffer curve (the relationship between tax rates and the amount of tax revenue collected by governments), with research pointing to the fact that higher equitability and compliance further increase compliance.

2.   Taxing Wealth

Wealth taxes, together with intergenerational taxes, are some of the most progressive tax measures. In OECD countries, wealth taxes contribute to nearly 2% of GDP on average, whereas they only play a marginal role in Asia. Their contribution is as high as 3.6% of GDP in Switzerland,[56] where all cantons levy a net wealth tax that includes bank account balances and investments, life insurances, vehicles, properties, and other valuables.[57] Other countries that have introduced wealth taxes include the Netherlands (*vermogensrendementheffing*), Spain (*patrimonio*), and France. The evidence on the effects of wealth taxes is debated, including their impact on entrepreneurship levels as well as consumption.[58] The evidence on the use of one-off taxes on wealth is less contested, indicating that they can be an effective measure at times of fiscal or economic distress. In fact, these taxes have been used in several instances to shore up public finances. Examples include Iceland (2009), Ireland (2011), and Cyprus (2013).[59] These taxes present the advantage that they have an immediate impact and can be designed to target individual income groups to maximize revenue mobilization without depressing consumption. Inheritance tax is a form of wealth tax on intergenerational transfers. It is common in OECD economies, but limited in the core countries, with only Thailand and the Philippines having measures in place. Administrative challenges, most notably disclosure and valuation, represent a key limitation to the potential impact of similar measures in the focus countries,[60] stressing the importance of a planning phase to maximize tax compliance as a precondition for their rollout.

[52]   Philippines Comprehensive Tax Reform Program. https://taxreform.dof.gov.ph/tax-reform-packages/p1-train/.

[53]   D. Coady. 2018. *Creating fiscal space. Finance and Development.* December. https://www.imf.org/external/pubs/ft/fandd/2018/12/pdf/taxes-and-social-protection-coady.pdf.

[54]   IMF. 2019. Indonesia: Selected Issues. *IMF Country Report* No. 19/251. https://www.imf.org/~/media/Files/Publications/CR/2019/1IDNEA2019002.ashx.

[55]   IMF. 2020. *Fiscal Policies For Women's Economic Empowerment.* https://blogs.imf.org/2020/02/18/fiscal-policies-for-womens-economic-empowerment/.

[56]   M. Brulhart et al. 2019. *Wealth Taxation: The Swiss Experience.* https://voxeu.org/article/wealth-taxation-swiss-experience.

[57]   PWC. 2020. *Worldwide Tax Summaries.* https://taxsummaries.pwc.com/switzerland/individual/other-taxes.

[58]   OECD. 2018. *The Role and Design of Net Wealth Taxes in the OECD.* https://doi.org/10.1787/9789264290303-en.

[59]   N. O'Donovan. 2020. *One-off Wealth Taxes: Theory and Evidence.* https://www.wealthandpolicy.com/wp/EP7_OneOff.pdf.

[60]   ESCAP. 2017. *Prospects for Progressive Tax Reform in Asia and the Pacific.* https://www.unescap.org/sites/default/files/S2_Prospects_for_Progressive_Tax_Reform.pdf.

3. Taxing Property

Property taxation, if well designed, is regarded as one of the best forms of taxation for contributing to social equity because of its progressive nature; it is also advantageous because it is difficult to avoid, given the high visibility and immobility of land and buildings.[61] Several countries are looking into leveraging property tax as a means to expanding their tax base. For example, the Philippines' Package 3 of the Comprehensive Tax Reform Program focuses on Real Property Valuation Reform (currently awaiting on senate approval). ADB has been assisting governments such as Indonesia[62] and Cambodia[63] through both advisory support and the development of knowledge products to inform related initiatives. Several reform processes are ongoing, for example in Cambodia, whereas others are undergoing legislative approval, for example in the Philippines. Specifically, in the Philippines, ADB supported a local governance reform project seeking to establish a real property valuation and transactions system that centralizes valuation functions at the Bureau of Local Governance Finance, mitigating political pressure among local government units to keep taxable values of lands artificially low. Recent initiatives look to address common issues that governments in the region face, including poor system design, exemptions, incomplete property databases, and weak administration.[64]

4. Taxing Environmental Externalities

The Association of Southeast Asian Nations' (ASEAN) share of global emissions has risen from 3% to 4.4% between 2000 and 2018 and energy-related carbon emissions are expected to rise by as much as 61% between 2014 and 2025.[65] Despite significant environmental challenges and fiscal deficits in financing sustainable development, environmental tax regimes are limited. For instance, environmentally related tax revenues in the Philippines represented just 0.2% of GDP or 1.4% of total tax revenues in 2018, well below the OECD averages of 1.6% of GDP and 7.2% of total tax revenues.[66] Indonesia faces a similar shortfall, having the third-lowest tax rate on energy on an economy-wide basis in a ranking of 41 countries (including 34 OECD members).[67] Conversely, fossil fuels consumption subsidies are common. As of 2018, fossil fuel subsidies in Southeast Asia amounted to $35 billion (0.5% of GDP).[68] A key barrier to reforming these subsidies is the absence of a strong safety net to adequately protect the poor from rising energy prices, which should be considered in the context of similar reforms (footnote 53). While governments in countries such as Indonesia, the Philippines, and Thailand are speeding up efforts to establish domestic carbon finance markets for land-use emissions (similar to cap-and-trade systems) amid significant increase in commodity-production-related deforestation, progress has been slow.[69] Effective pricing of externalities presents a significant opportunity for governments to raise revenues while promoting a green transition, shifting the tax base from labor to resources. Germany, for example, introduced an ecological tax reform in 1999 that raised taxes on transport fuels, electricity, and heating fuels, while

[61] ADB. 2020. *Strengthening Property Tax Management to Enhance Local Revenue.* https://www.adb.org/sites/default/files/project-documents/54076/54076-001-tar-en.pdf.

[62] ADB. 2019. *Country Operations Business Plan. Indonesia 2020–2022.* https://www.adb.org/sites/default/files/institutional-document/526266/cobp-ino-2020-2022.pdf.

[63] ADB. 2020. *Cambodia's Property Tax Reform: Policy Considerations Toward Sustained Revenue Mobilization.* https://www.adb.org/sites/default/files/publication/561136/governance-brief-038-cambodia-property-tax-reform.pdf ; and ADB. 2020. *Strengthening Property Tax Management to Enhance Local Revenue.* https://www.adb.org/sites/default/files/project-documents/54076/54076-001-tar-en.pdf.

[64] ADB. 2020. *Cambodia's Property Tax Reform: Policy Considerations Toward Sustained Revenue Mobilization.* https://www.adb.org/sites/default/files/publication/561136/governance-brief-038-cambodia-property-tax-reform.pdf.

[65] ASEAN Secretariat. 2018. *Fifth ASEAN State of the Environment Report (SOER5).* Brunei Darussalam. https://environment.asean.org/soer5/; and S. Sandu et al. 2019. Energy-related CO$_2$ Emissions Growth in ASEAN Countries: Trends, Drivers, and Policy Implications. *Energies.* 12. p. 4650. https://doi.org/10.3390/en12244650.

[66] OECD. 2020. *Environmental Taxation.* https://www.oecd.org/environment/environmentaltaxation.htm.

[67] OECD Centre for Tax Policy and Administration. 2020. *Environmentally-Related Taxes—Taxes on Energy Use in Indonesia.* https://www.oecd.org/indonesia/environmental-tax-profile-indonesia.pdf.

[68] International Energy Agency, as quoted in Robin Hicks. 2019. Southeast Asia's Dependence on Fossil Fuel Subsidies "Like Crack Cocaine". *Eco-Business.* https://www.eco-business.com/news/southeast-asias-dependence-on-fossil-fuel-subsidies-like-crack-cocaine/#:~:text=Fossil%20fuel%20subsidies%20in,decade%2C%20to%202.8%20per%20cent.

[69] J. Aleluia. 2019. *Carbon Pricing in Southeast Asia—Current Status and Future Perspectives.* Manila: UNFCCC/IGES Regional Collaboration Centre—Bangkok. https://unfccc.int/sites/default/files/resource/Session%202%20Joao%20Aleluia.pdf.

simultaneously reducing the cost of labor by reducing social security contributions. According to the German Institute for Economic Research, the reforms created up to 250,000 additional jobs in Germany in the first 4 years after its adoption.[70]

5. Taxing Digital Services

Estimates of the size of the digital economy range from 4.5% to 15.5% of world GDP.[71] As the digital sector emerges as a key growth engine, particularly in Thailand, Indonesia, and the Philippines, identifying tax models that balance revenue collection and support of sector growth represents a significant opportunity. Under current regulations, corporations are taxed based on where production occurs, rather than where products are consumed, which presents a challenge for the taxation of digital services. Initiatives to capitalize on this opportunity are already underway. At the global level, international cooperation pertaining to the taxation of the digital economy is progressing under the OECD/G20 Inclusive Framework on BEPS, which groups 137 countries and jurisdictions for multilateral negotiation of international tax rules.[72] At a national level, some countries have taken unilateral steps. For example, Indonesia has introduced Government Regulation in Lieu of Law Number 1 Year 2020 (Perppu-1) (subsequently converted into law), which regulates taxation of the digital economy through both direct tax (income tax) and indirect tax (VAT) obligations on foreign sellers, service providers, and foreign e-commerce platforms (foreign digital players).[73] The tax has been reported to have generated Rp297 billion ($21 million) from selected technology companies and e-commerce platforms to October 2020 and its contribution is expected to expand as more companies are appointed as VAT collectors.[74] A similar initiative is ongoing in the Philippines, where proposed measures identify digital service providers' VAT registration requirements with gross sales or receipts exceeding ₱3 million ($62,000) over the previous 12 months.[75] Tax administrations that are pursuing these initiatives are looking to strike a balance between achieving immediate results from a revenue mobilization perspective while advancing domestic policies that align with global tax initiatives. Care must be taken with such unilateral approaches as if poorly designed it could jeopardize growth in the digital economy, and lead to reciprocal action from overseas markets that could potentially lose on their share of tax revenues. Some of the key challenges that policy makers will need to tackle to effectively set up such taxes include the capacity of the administration to monitor online transactions, determining location of consumption, accounting for tax preferences, registration of vendors, and distribution of responsibilities in VAT remittance.

B.   Increasing Tax Compliance

Tax compliance is low in all core countries due to a combination of high levels of informality, VAT fraud, and tax avoidance (Table 4). Increasing tax compliance can enable countries to maximize the contribution of existing taxes by ensuring that all transactions are covered. Challenges range from upstream issues such as ensuring that individuals and businesses are registered as taxpayers to downstream issues pertaining to tax evasion and fraud. Approaches to address these issues vary in complexity, reach, and nature, offering combinations of policy and operational measures, including leveraging emerging technologies. An important consideration in

---

[70]   E. Von Weizsäcker et al. 2009. *Factor Five: Transforming the Global Economy Through 80% Improvements in Resource Productivity.* London: Earthscan.

[71]   UNCTAD. 2019. *Digital Economy Report.* https://unctad.org/system/files/official-document/der2019_overview_en.pdf.

[72]   OECD. 2019a. http://www.oecd.org/tax/beps/inclusive-framework-on-beps-composition.pdf (Figures refer to December 2019).

[73]   International Tax Review. 2020. *Taxing the Digital Economy in Indonesia.* https://www.internationaltaxreview.com/article/b1ngz37n2ts6ct/taxing-the-digital-economy-in-indonesia.

[74]   *The Jakarta Post.* 2020. Indonesia Collects $20.9m in Digital Tax as of October. https://www.thejakartapost.com/news/2020/11/24/indonesia-collects-20-9m-in-digital-tax-as-of-october.html.

[75]   A. Tionko. 2020. Tax Enforcement in Digital Economy and Digital Transformation in Tax Administration: The Philippine Experience. Presentation at the Southeast Asia Symposium on Domestic Resource Mobilization for COVID 19 Economic Recovery, Asian Development Bank. 1–3 December 2020.

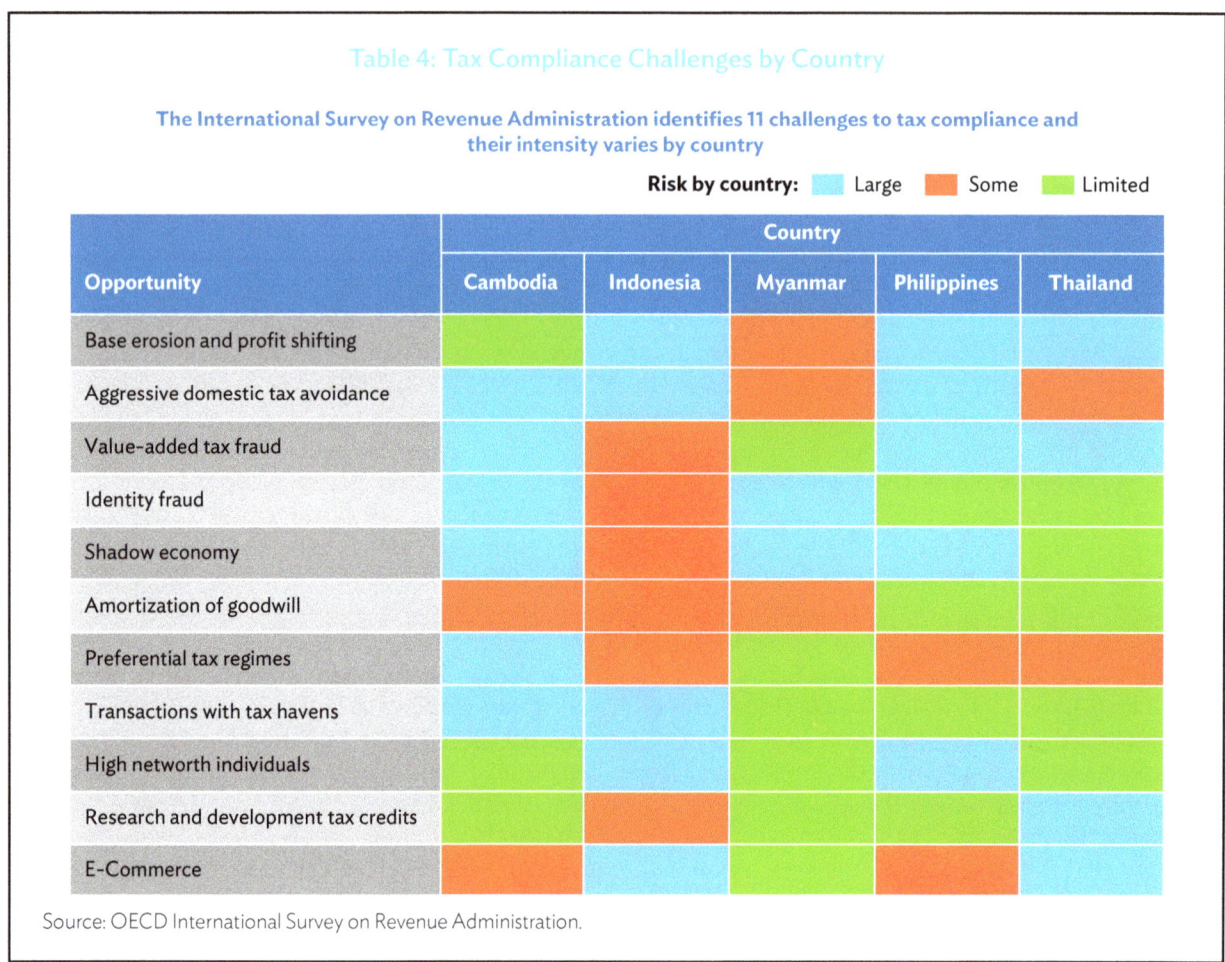

Table 4: Tax Compliance Challenges by Country

The International Survey on Revenue Administration identifies 11 challenges to tax compliance and their intensity varies by country

Risk by country: ▮ Large ▮ Some ▮ Limited

Opportunity	Country				
	Cambodia	Indonesia	Myanmar	Philippines	Thailand
Base erosion and profit shifting	Limited	Large	Some	Large	Large
Aggressive domestic tax avoidance	Large	Large	Some	Large	Some
Value-added tax fraud	Large	Some	Limited	Large	Large
Identity fraud	Large	Large	Some	Limited	Limited
Shadow economy	Large	Large	Large	Large	Limited
Amortization of goodwill	Some	Large	Large	Limited	Limited
Preferential tax regimes	Large	Some	Limited	Some	Some
Transactions with tax havens	Large	Large	Limited	Limited	Limited
High networth individuals	Limited	Large	Limited	Large	Large
Research and development tax credits	Limited	Some	Large	Limited	Large
E-Commerce	Some	Large	Some	Large	Limited

Source: OECD International Survey on Revenue Administration.

the selection of measures that address compliance issues (and tax administration more broadly) is around their return on investment. As countries are set to continue facing fiscal sustainability pressures due to economic growth constraints and uncertainty, investment in reform programs will need to be carefully evaluated. Global benchmarks offer some examples of return on investment assessments on individual measures (particularly technology solutions). However, prioritizing interventions will need contextualization of these assessments and will need to account for potentially prolonged fiscal constraints. Considerations around readiness offer an important framework to guide these decisions (these are discussed in the final section of this report).

1.   Shrinking the Informal Economy

Taxing the informal sector has been linked to accelerating growth of firms in the formal economy, sustaining tax morale, improving governance, and expanding the tax base.[76] Besides limiting tax revenue, informality presents a challenge to effective tax expenditure and welfare, as unregistered individuals fail to benefit from social protection measures. Increasing compliance levels of both individuals and businesses can substantially expand tax revenue, while driving better social equity outcomes. Registering individuals and businesses as taxpayers is a critical first step, and an enabler to further measures to increase their tax compliance. Aadhaar, the world's largest biometric identity project, which India rolled out in 2009, is the largest initiative to bring individuals into the formal economy. Aadhaar is used for

---

[76]   A. Joshi et al. 2012. Taxing the Informal Economy: Challenges, Possibilities and Remaining Questions. *ICTD Working Paper* 4. https://opendocs. ids.ac.uk/opendocs/bitstream/handle/20.500.12413/2309/ICTD%20Working%20Paper%204.pdf.

security purposes in many government and private sector applications, including pensions, wages, and the distribution of benefits. The use of individual identification numbers is now being mandated for income tax returns, effectively linking access to individual services to the establishment of a tax identity (footnote 34). At the corporate level, governments have trialed measures to mainstream tax registration, for example by linking it to business registration. Thailand has introduced a regulatory reform that requires new businesses to submit a company income tax identity card if they are looking to register.[77] Downstream measures include the use of data techniques to retrieve insights from mass amounts of unstructured data. Data can be analyzed and mapped to declared income by taxpayers to identify potential discrepancies. Tax intelligence software can help reduce leakage by identifying high risk cases such that audit resources could be used more efficiently. The United Kingdom uses a product called COSAIN that automates the collation and filtering of social media and websites. India's Project Insight relies on social media postings to match residents' spending patterns with their declared income. Italy uses a tool called Redditometro—a data analytical tool that examines a taxpayer's expenditure patterns against where they live and the type of household they are in. Cases flagged for inconsistencies would warrant a closer examination of the taxpayer's tax returns.

Some progress has been made on these issues in the focus countries. At the corporate level, rationalization efforts that bring together tax registration with other administrative requirements can be a boon to compliance and have been implemented by all core countries in recent years, the latest being Cambodia,[78] Myanmar,[79] and Thailand.[80] Cambodia's online Single Portal for business registrations (in English and Khmer) aims to approve registrations within 8 working days and links business registration, tax registration, and a dedicated bank account. Rationalization efforts should be complemented by taxpayer education and assistance programs, as taxpayers cannot comply if they do not understand their obligations. High levels of informality call for similar programs and global examples point to the use of educational platforms, use of testimonials, public holidays (e.g., national tax days), bookkeeping workshops, media campaigns, and use of social media, among others.[81] Prevalence of tax identification numbers is low and educational initiatives can also be tied to enrollment initiatives. Mobile applications offer an opportunity to reach rural segments of the population and have been trialed only by Thailand and the Philippines to date (footnote 19). Other relevant approaches to expand the PIT base include direct engagement with employers and the introduction of prefilled tax returns or "pay-as-you-earn" withholding regimes. In addition to active measures that seek to streamline the tax registration process, voluntary compliance is highly dependent on citizens' confidence that institutions will spend tax revenue effectively and that penalties will be applied in the case of noncompliance. Measures designed to promote perceptions of trust and fairness in the tax administration and the tax system have been strongly linked to improvements in compliance.[82]

---

[77] Thailand Board of Investment. *Setting Up a Business.* https://www.boi.go.th/index.php?page=setting_up_a_business.

[78] ASEAN Briefing. 2020. *Cambodia Launches New Online Business Registration System.* https://www.aseanbriefing.com/news/cambodia-launches-new-online-business-registration-system/.

[79] DFDL. 2020. *Myanmar: IRD Introduces E-Filing System & Expands E-Payment Platforms to Taxpayers.* https://www.dfdl.com/resources/legal-and-tax-updates/myanmar-ird-introduced-e-filing-system-expands-e-payment-platforms-to-taxpayers/.

[80] Thailand Board of Investment. *Setting Up a Business.* https://www.boi.go.th/index.php?page=setting_up_a_business.

[81] OECD. 2015. *Building Tax Culture, Compliance and Citizenship: A Global Source Book on Taxpayer Education.* https://doi.org/10.1787/9789264205154-en.

[82] A. Chooi. 2020. *Improving Tax Compliance.* ADB Governance Brief 39/2020. https://www.adb.org/sites/default/files/publication/562431/governance-brief-039-improving-tax-compliance.pdf.

2.   Tackling Value-Added Tax Fraud

VAT fraud involves activities such as failure of businesses to register, underreporting or suppression of sales, misclassification of supplies to the effect of applying a reduced rate, failure to account for VAT on transactions, and smuggling goods into the country, among other measures.[83] Given the large size of the informal sector in all five core countries, tackling VAT fraud is especially important from a revenue-gathering perspective. It is also an important element in tax reforms that seek to transition from tax breaks and tax holidays to tax credits and deductions, which are desirable from both a compliance and a tax base expansion standpoint. Opportunities to address this vary in terms of complexity. Data recording technologies, referred to as fiscal control units in some countries, help to secure sales data in point of sales systems so that tampering by phantomware or zappers can be prevented. In Hungary, fiscal control units were installed in electronic cash registers used in sectors concerned, such as hospitality. Within a year, VAT revenues rose by 15%, an amount, which already exceeded the cost of implementation. Belgium reported an 8% increase in reported restaurant sales after installation of the technology.[84]

Implementation in the focus countries would be reliant on a series of conditions: enforcement, availability of technology, and internet connectivity. Identifying how gaps would hinder the realization of the full benefits these technologies offer would be a critical step in the evaluation of their return on investment. The growth of the digital economy, and in particular online sales, has created additional complexity and increased the risks of underreporting, as it is difficult for tax administrations to know when and where a sale has been made.[85] E-invoicing methods are used by trading partners, such as customers and their suppliers, to present and monitor transactional documents between one another and ensure the terms of their trading agreements are being met. E-invoicing creates a trail of digitized transaction details that can be used to track under declaration of revenues for tax purposes by businesses. Many countries in Latin America have compulsory e-invoicing laws. The European Commission also issued a directive for the mandatory implementation of an European Union-wide electronic invoicing network. In Mexico, e-invoicing led to growth in income tax (6% for businesses and 21% for individuals), while bringing 4.2 million MSMEs previously undetected by the tax authority into the formal economy.[86] Other impact estimates show that there is a decline in VAT dodging from 32% in 2011 to 19% in 2015.[87] Real-time VAT reporting is a specific form of e-invoicing where companies are mandated to report necessary information in each invoice to the tax authorities in digital format. According to software services company Tieto and Finnish Financial Services, adopting a uniform standard could increase European tax revenues by €160 billion annually. In Spain, it is now compulsory for large payers to file their VAT information in real time on the new online system known as Suministro Inmediato de Información.[88] At the cutting edge, the application of blockchain to tax functions has a huge potential impact for tracking and monitoring taxable assets as well as transactions. If ownership and location of digital assets were reliably captured at asset creation and updated throughout their lifetime, opportunities for tax evasion would decrease.[89] For example, Thailand's Revenue Department has been testing blockchain to track VAT payments in its innovation lab, with a particular focus on VAT refund fraud.[90]

---

[83]   M. Walpole. 2014. *Tackling VAT Fraud. International VAT Monitor September/October 2014.* https://www.ibfd.org/shop/international-tackling-vat-fraud.

[84]   OECD. 2016. *Technologies for Better Tax Administration: A Practical Guide for Revenue Bodies.* Paris: OECD Publishing. https://read.oecd-ilibrary.org/taxation/technologies-for-better-tax-administration_9789264256439-en#page4.

[85]   R. de La Feria and A. Schoeman. 2019. Addressing VAT Fraud in Developing Countries: The Tax Policy-Administration Symbiosis. *Intertax.* 47 (11). pp. 950–967. https://ssrn.com/abstract=3481861 or https://doi.org/10.2139/ssrn.3481861.

[86]   OECD. 2017. *Technology Tools to Tackle Tax Evasion and Tax Fraud.* https://www.oecd.org/tax/crime/technology-tools-to-tackle-tax-evasion-and-tax-fraud.pdf.

[87]   EDICOM. 2017. *Impact of CFDI on Tax Evasion.* http://cfdi.edicomgroup.com/en/cfdi-al-dia-en/impact-cfdi-tax-evasion/.

[88]   DLA Piper. 2017. *Spain Requires Real-Time Submissions of VAT Information.* https://www.dlapiper.com/en/us/insights/publications/2017/07/spain-requires-vat-information/.

[89]   PwC. 2016. *How Blockchain Technology Could Improve the Tax System.* https://www.pwc.co.uk/issues/futuretax/assets/documents/how-blockchain-could-improve-the-tax-system.pdf.

[90]   *Bangkok Post.* 2018. Blockchain Undergoes Tests for Tracking VAT Payments. 3 December. https://www.bangkokpost.com/business/1586614/blockchain-undergoes-tests-for-tracking-vat-payments.

C.   Improving Tax Administration

Several tax collection agencies globally have begun a transition toward e-administration, with increased options and uptake of online filing of tax returns, online payments, and the full or partial prefilling of tax returns.[91] Complexity is a key barrier to tax compliance. A 2017 Deloitte survey suggests that tax compliance and reporting obligations are deemed complicated by businesses, with the share of respondents indicating so averaging over 80% in the focus countries (Cambodia was not included in the assessment) (footnote 23). This is a particularly significant challenge for MSMEs, which have limited administrative resources. Tax administrations can consider initiatives to make online lodgment simpler, easing the tax payment process, and enhancing communication with taxpayers.

1.   Making Online Lodgment Simple

Globally, there has been a significant shift toward e-administration with increasing options for online filing of tax returns. According to the International Survey on Revenue Administration (a multiorganization international survey to collect national-level information and data on tax administration), e-filing rates for PIT are now above 70% and those for corporate income tax are around 85% in the administrations part of the assessment. However, filing taxes is still a time-consuming activity in the focus countries. On average, businesses need 209 hours to comply with tax requirements, a performance level above the global average of 234, but a long way from Bahrain's 22.5 hours. While global comparisons can miss contextual factors, they provide an interesting benchmark to identify potential gaps. In fact, they point to a significant opportunity to both decrease the burden of tax compliance and to lower the barrier to entry for individuals or businesses that do not file taxes because it is too complicated. Well-designed tax portals can allow taxpayers to file their return, track their refunds, make online payments, obtain a copy of their prior year's return or income details to access other services, and be able to do all this through one single access account. Increasing the convenience to taxpayers through integrated services helps to improve tax compliance (footnote 84). In Singapore, User Experience Design has been adopted in redesigning the "myTax Portal" for use on desktop and mobile. Prepopulated tax returns can also reduce leakage by reducing the risk of noncompliance and contact between taxpayer and revenue authority, reducing the scope for corruption and other leakages. According to interviewees, several developed countries such as Singapore and Estonia have very efficient auto filing tax systems, drawing from a broad range of data from different ministries to reduce the filing requirements of taxpayers.

2.   Easing Payment Processes

As of 2019 in Myanmar, the average amount of time spent to comply with tax administration requirements is 282 hours per year. Part of this time is spent physically visiting the tax office to pay in person with cash or cheques. The country has rolled out an e-payment system that makes it mandatory for Yangon-based companies to pay income tax, commercial tax, or special commodity tax through a mobile payment system.[92] This is part of a global trend, whereby different forms of digital payments (i.e., internet banking, mobile payments, direct debit, etc.) are used to increase the convenience for payers and lower the risk of late or nonpayment. Providing means for taxpayers (both individuals and corporates) to conveniently settle their obligations using internet banking portals have led to more timely receipts. One example is in Malaysia where Citibank Berhad and Lembaga Hasil Dalam Negeri Malaysia launched CitiConnectSM e-Tax—an online payment solution that allows firms to settle their tax payments to Lembaga Hasil Dalam Negeri Malaysia.[93] Multichannel access can also provide significant

[91]   OECD. 2019. *Tax Administration 2019: Comparative Information on OECD and other Advanced and Emerging Economies.* https://doi.org/10.1787/74d162b6-en.

[92]   *Myanmar Times.* 2020. All Yangon Firms Must Use e-Tax Payment by October. 17 August. https://www.mmtimes.com/news/all-yangon-firms-must-use-e-tax-payment-october.html.

[93]   Citigroup. 2009. *Citibank and LHDNM Launch e-Tax Payment.* http://www.citigroup.com/citi/news/2009/090529a.htm.

benefits, particularly where taxpayers have different levels of proficiency with digital platforms. For example, Thailand's new tax payment options include ATM, counter services, internet banking, mobile banking, credit and debit card payment, QR codes, and a tax smart card.[94]

3.   Enhancing Communication with Taxpayers

Ensuring that tax administrations are accessible, transparent, and engaged presents short-term opportunities to support tax compliance and long-term opportunities to improve tax culture. Education of taxpayers can support them in gaining a better understanding of their obligations and raising awareness on the role of tax in society (footnote 91). For example, in Singapore, Inland Revenue Authority of Singapore uses a short message service to communicate policy changes to taxpayers and also to send reminders for filing and payment. A total of 6 million messages were sent in 2015 and more than 96% of those surveyed agreed that the short message service was timely and helpful. Inland Revenue Department in New Zealand started sending text reminders in 2016, a practice that is becoming increasingly common in developing and emerging economies. Social media outlets such as Twitter and Facebook are used to communicate policy changes and deadline reminders. The United Kingdom's HM Revenue and Customs has set up a social media customer support team that uses a range of social media including Twitter, Facebook, Instagram, YouTube, and LinkedIn to disseminate news and updates, and provide guidance, and answer questions from the public. The engagement is intended to complement formal communication channels by the HM Revenue and Customs.[95] Examples of innovative approaches that focus on education include France's effort to explain in practical terms how individuals' tax revenue is used through a simulator, Georgia's "Let's pay for a better future" (targeting students), and Japan's cooperation with industry groups within the sharing economy sector to disseminate tax knowledge among individuals who are to file a tax return for the first time (footnote 91).

▶   Prioritizing the Interventions: What Could Have the Greatest Impact?

An important question is which of the identified areas offers the greatest promise and what countries should be focusing on. To understand the potential impact of interventions, AlphaBeta sized the potential benefits from a revenue collection standpoint of interventions in 6 of the 10 areas discussed above: increasing PIT progressivity, taxing wealth, taxing property, environmental taxation, taxing digital services, and curbing VAT fraud (Table 5). The approach is informed by the recorded impact of similar interventions in benchmark economies as well as by an assessment of the potential benefit deriving from closing the gap relative to regional and global benchmarks.[96] This bottom-up assessment points to a potential upside opportunity of $84 billion on an annual basis for the five focus economies. Interestingly, environmental taxation emerges as the most significant opportunity, followed by property taxation. While it is not feasible that countries will make these full reforms to capture the available potential in 1 year, this assessment offers an interesting thought experiment to inform the prioritization of different tax reforms.

---

[94]   E. Nitithanprapas. Presentation at the Southeast Asia Symposium on Domestic Resource Mobilization for COVID 19 Economic Recovery. Asian Development Bank. 1–3 December 2020.

[95]   For more information, please refer to: https://www.gov.uk/government/organisations/hm-revenue-customs/about/social-media-use#why-hmrc-engages-in-social-media.

[96]   The methodology and assumptions are discussed in detail in the Appendix.

Table 5: Sizing the Potential Impact of Interventions

Opportunities to enhance the tax base and enhance tax compliance could lead to additional tax revenues of $84 billion annually if fully implemented

Improvement opportunity by country: Large   Some   Limited

Opportunity ($ Million)		Country					Total
		Cambodia	Indonesia	Myanmar	Philippines	Thailand	
Expanding the base	Increasing PIT progressivity	81	3,417	215	1,154	1,679	6,547
	Taxing wealth	81	3,417	215	1,154	1,679	6,547
	Taxing property	269	15,947	1,006	4,231	6,157	27,610
	Environmental taxation	359	15,178	957	4,461	8,621	29,576
	Taxing digital services	40	1,732	15	456	945	3,188
Enhancing compliance	Curbing VAT fraud	270	4,938	217	1,295	3,947	10,852
	Total	1,100	44,629	2,626	12,751	23,028	84,132

PIT = personal income tax, VAT = value- added tax.
Note: Based on analysis of existing policies in these areas. Sizing may not be reflective of scale of opportunity relative to existing policies, e.g., for PIT, it is assumed that all countries gain additional tax revenues sized at 0.3% in gross domestic product in 2019. See methodology for further details.
Sources: AlphaBeta analysis; Asian Development Bank; International Monetary Fund; Literature review; World Bank.

D.   Supporting International Tax Cooperation

Perceptions about equity in the distribution of tax burden are important in strengthening overall community confidence in the tax system. One way to bolster these perceptions is to demonstrate effective supervision over the wealthiest taxpayers in the community, particularly multinational enterprises and high-wealth and high-income individuals, who are often perceived by the general community to engage in aggressive tax planning, including the use of international profit shifting, to minimize their taxation. Effective supervision of these taxpayers depends on a number of factors including domestic legal frameworks and the capacity of the revenue body (footnote 16).

SECTION IV

Conclusion

Domestic resource mobilization is a critical component of COVID-19 recovery strategies in Southeast Asia. It is an important element in the Asian Development Bank's Strategy 2030 and can contribute to several of its operational priorities.[97] For example, fair and efficient tax systems are critical to **addressing poverty and reducing inequalities** and considerations around progressivity and inclusiveness will be particularly important as countries account for equity considerations in tax reform initiatives post-COVID. Tax reform can be used to **accelerate progress in gender equality**, for example, by taxing individuals rather than households, an intervention that has demonstrated to support women empowerment. Environmental taxation can contribute to **tackling climate change, building climate and disaster resilience, and enhancing environmental sustainability**. Reforms that streamline the use of digital technology in tax administration and simplify tax compliance can contribute to **strengthening governance and institutional capacity**. Finally, international cooperation, for example on BEPS, can help **foster regional cooperation and integration**. As countries transition from response to recovery, opportunities to optimize taxation will offer an important contribution to the broader advancement of their economies and societies.

Before implementing the outlined recommendations, governments should distinguish between "low-hanging fruits" that they can capture in the near term versus policies that require longer timeframes to implement and take effect. Countries should take into account multiple factors, including the policy's potential for short-term impact and its political feasibility. For instance, carbon taxes have proven politically difficult to implement in many countries.

A further important consideration is understanding the readiness of countries to implement certain tax reforms. For example, implementing a property tax requires certain prerequisites such as land registries and a cadaster (i.e., an institution conducting land surveys and providing legal information relating to real estate). Table 6 provides an overview of the implementing measures for each of the 10 recommendations based on readiness levels. For some countries, the focus should be on "basic readiness" measures that relate to foundational reforms needed. For other countries that are at an "advanced readiness" stage, the implementing measures focus on more complex or additive interventions to fully capture the opportunity. Often, the ideal strategy will involve a mix of both basic and advanced measures, as countries have the opportunity to leverage areas where they have an existing advantage. For example, broadening PIT through increased tax progressivity could begin with rationalizing tax deductions. Reforms in this direction are part of the Philippines' TRAIN reform program and are currently under consideration in Thailand.[98] Similarly for taxing wealth, a starting point could be to focus on just high-wealth individuals, potentially with the establishment of a dedicated unit within large taxpayer offices.

For taxation of property, a starting point could be to address cadastral record-keeping issues (e.g., interoperability across government agencies) while expanding tax coverage beyond the limited subset of local administrations where they exist (if they exist at all) today. A related challenge is around the interaction between local

---

[97] ADB. 2018. *Strategy 2030: Achieving a Prosperous, Inclusive, Resilient, and Sustainable Asia and the Pacific.* Manila. https://www.adb.org/sites/default/files/institutional-document/435391/strategy-2030-main-document.pdf.

[98] *The Bangkok Post.* 2020. Deduction Incentives to be Reviewed. 8 December. https://www.bangkokpost.com/business/2031719/deduction-incentives-to-be-reviewed.

Table 6: Implementing Measures for Each Recommendation by Readiness Level

The implementing measures for the 10 recommendations will vary depending on each country's readiness level

	Basic Readiness Measures	Advanced Readiness Measures
1. Broadening PIT progressivity	• Rationalize tax deductions regimes • Understand relative burden of PIT on income groups • Ensure baseline level of PIT registrations	• Explore advanced data analytics for PIT reporting
Country relevance	CAM, MYA	INO, PHI, THA
2. Taxing wealth	• Establish a high net wealth unit within the large taxpayer office • Ensure financial data transparency and database interoperability • Ensure baseline level of PIT registrations	• Operationalize OECD Standard for Automatic Exchange of Information • Introduce data science and big data analytics for tax fraud detection
Country relevance	CAM, MYA	INO, PHI, THA
3. Taxing property	• Introduce cadaster registries • Introduce land registration system • Rationalize tax exemptions • Ensure data transparency between local authorities and tax dept	• Trial geographic information system technologies to enhance compliance • Develop property market transaction data to enhance valuations and transparency
Country relevance	CAM, INO, MYA, PHI, THA	
4. Environmental taxation	• Rationalize fuel subsidies • Explore direct taxation of fuel imports	• Design emission trading systems • Design and introduce taxation on environmentally harmful products
Country relevance	CAM, INO, MYA	PHI, THA
5. Taxing the digital economy	• Conduct industry consultations and secure alignment; assess impact on sector competitiveness • Participate in OECD BEPS proceedings	• Use data science and big data analytics to capture micro, small, and medium-sized enterprises digital sales • Harmonize domestic regulations with BEPS developments
Country relevance	CAM, MYA	INO, PHI, THA
6. Shrinking the informal economy	• Develop encompassing taxpayer databases with unique tax identification numbers • Tie business registration to tax registration • Drive (digital) financial inclusion over basic threshold	• Develop national identification platforms that combine unique identification with financial information • Explore big data analytics to process unstructured data for compliance • Develop pay-as-you-earn withholding regimes with employers • Introduce "digital payment platforms by default"
Country relevance	CAM, MYA	INO, PHI, THA
7. Trackling VAT fraud	• Rationalize tax credits claim process • Introduce data recording technologies to help to secure sales data in point-of-sale systems	• Introduce mandatory e-invoicing and real-time VAT reporting • Leverage big data to audit corporate tax declarations • Use blockchain technology for tracking and monitoring of assets and transactions
Country relevance	CAM, MYA	INO, PHI, THA
8. Making tax lodgment simple	• Introduce online tax portals (including apps) • Achieve high levels of digital literacy	• Ensure online tax portals platform interoperability through user experience design • Roll-out pre-populated tax returns • Introduce e-services to support self-service in tax lodgment
Country relevance	CAM, MYA	INO, PHI, THA
9. Easing the payment process	• Introduce multi-channel payment methods (in-person and digital)	• Develop online systems to resolve mismatches in tax returns • Develop automatic payment and refund systems
Country relevance		CAM, INO, MYA, PHI, THA
10. Enhancing tax communication	• Mainstream mobile and online methods to communicate with taxpayers • Balance tax education campaigns spanning physical and digital	• Use big data to identify person-to-person transaction and educating on tax obligations • Co-create tax portals with taxpayers
Country relevance	CAM, INO, MYA, PHI	THA

CAM = Cambodia, BEPS = base erosion and profit shifting, INO = Indonesia, MYA = Myanmar, OECD = Organisation for Economic Co-operation and Development, PHI = Philippines, PIT = personal income tax, THA = Thailand, VAT = value-added tax.
Sources: Various; AlphaBeta analysis.

administrations, which are responsible for property tax collection, and central administration, particularly the revenue department: linking separate systems would provide greater oversight on individuals' fiscal positions. The Philippines' reform centralizing valuation functions at the Bureau of Local Governance Finance offers an interesting blueprint for other countries to explore. More advanced measures could include investment in the development of listings and online registries that collect transaction data, which would provide transparency for both tax authorities and buyers and enhance valuation processes, an important issue as property markets in the focus countries are still developing and cash transactions and underreporting are common.

With regard to environmental taxation, this can be a politically challenging area. A starting point could be to reduce fuel subsidies and increase taxation when oil prices are low.[99] For example, the Philippines temporarily imposed a 10% import duty on crude oil and refined petroleum products to raise government funds for its COVID-19 response.[100]

For digital taxation, a starting point would be to engage closely with industry to understand their perspectives, sizing the potential opportunity (particularly given the analysis highlighted earlier suggests the potential for tax revenue is far less than other measures), and consider how to mitigate potential risks (e.g., retaliatory taxation measures from other countries). Table 6 provides further examples of measures by readiness levels for the other recommendations.

[99]   C. Abdallah et al. 2020. *The Time Is Right! Reforming Fuel Product Pricing Under Low Oil Prices. IMF Special Series on COVID-19.* https://www.imf.org/-/media/Files/Publications/covid19-special-notes/enspecial-series-on-covid19the-time-is-right-reforming-fuel-product-pricing-under-low-oil-prices.ashx.
[100] Vivid Economics. 2020. *Greenness of Stimulus Index.* https://www.vivideconomics.com/casestudy/greenness-for-stimulus-index/ and R. A. Gita-Carlos. 2020. Increased Tariffs on Imported Oil Products Temporary: Palace. *Philippine News Agency.* https://www.pna.gov.ph/articles/1102775.

Methodology for Sizing Tax Revenue Potential

This appendix provides a brief overview of the methodology used in the quantitative analysis for sizing the tax revenue potential.

▶ Potential fiscal impact of tax reforms.

To illustrate the potential impact of tax reforms on each of the focus countries in this study, both a "top-down" and a "bottom-up" methodology have been used:

- **Top-down methodology.** This is used to provide an illustration of the overall ambition that focus countries can look to for expanding their tax revenues. Accordingly, it considers total tax revenues, expressed as a share of gross domestic product (GDP), and how this ratio can increase over the forecast period 2020–2025 if countries in Southeast Asia could match the historical increase of the top performing Asian Development Bank (ADB) members over the past 5 years of available data. The cumulative size of the increase in tax revenues over 2020–2025 is measured.

- **Bottom-up methodology.** This is used to provide an indication of the largest individual opportunities to expand the tax base and increase tax compliance, i.e., increasing personal income tax (PIT) progressivity, taxing wealth, taxing property, environmental taxation, taxing digital services, and curbing value-added tax (VAT) fraud. Each opportunity was sized individually for the five focus countries—Cambodia, .Indonesia, Myanmar, the Philippines, and Thailand. The size of the opportunity is expressed in terms of additional tax revenues that can be achieved in 1 year based on the latest available data on tax revenues and GDP.

▶ Top-Down Methodology—Sizing Tax-to-GDP Potential

This exercise forecasts the cumulative increase in tax revenues for economies in Southeast Asia over 2020–2025.[1] It relies on the tax-to-GDP indicator, which expresses the total tax revenues in an economy as a share of the GDP in any given year. Tax-to-GDP ratios vary significantly for economies with different underlying market characteristics, stages of economic development, and tax regimes. For instance, developed economies typically have higher tax-to-GDP ratios than developing economies, and these remain relatively stable over long periods of time. However, economies with larger public sectors, such as those with large welfare states, tend to have higher tax-to-GDP ratios—irrespective of their level of economic development.

---

[1] This forecast includes Cambodia, Indonesia, the Lao People's Democratic Republic (Lao PDR), Myanmar, the Philippines, Thailand, and Viet Nam. It excludes Brunei Darussalam and Singapore as they have graduated from regular ADB assistance. It also excludes Timor-Leste because of tax revenue data volatility, which restricts the ability to make informed tax forecasts.

Three steps were applied in this calculation:

- **Step 1—Analysis of regional performance.** Economies were split into two groups for this analysis—those with tax-to-GDP ratios above and below 15% in the latest year of available data. For economies in each category, we assessed the growth rates in tax-to-GDP ratios of the top 10 performers over the past 5 years of available data from the World Bank.[2] Those with a ratio greater than 15% grew on average by 1.8% over the 5-year period, while those with ratios below 15% grew on average 2.44% over the 5-year period (see Figure A1).

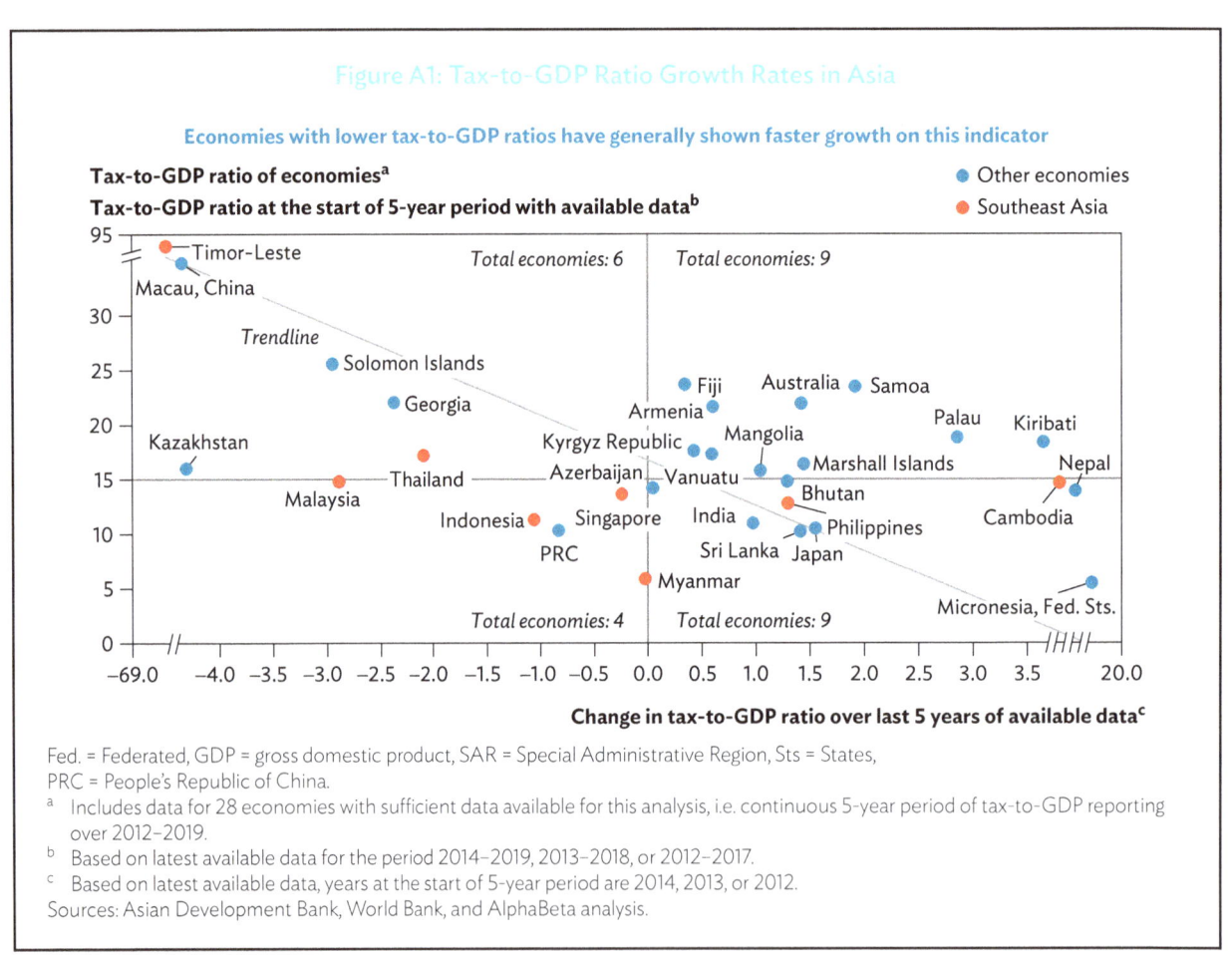

Figure A1: Tax-to-GDP Ratio Growth Rates in Asia

Economies with lower tax-to-GDP ratios have generally shown faster growth on this indicator

Fed. = Federated, GDP = gross domestic product, SAR = Special Administrative Region, Sts = States, PRC = People's Republic of China.

[a] Includes data for 28 economies with sufficient data available for this analysis, i.e. continuous 5-year period of tax-to-GDP reporting over 2012–2019.

[b] Based on latest available data for the period 2014–2019, 2013–2018, or 2012–2017.

[c] Based on latest available data, years at the start of 5-year period are 2014, 2013, or 2012.

Sources: Asian Development Bank, World Bank, and AlphaBeta analysis.

- **Step 2—Forecast for Southeast Asia.** These growth rates were then applied to the Southeast Asian countries considered in this analysis for the forecast period of 2020–2025. Countries with tax-to-GDP ratios in 2020[3] were similarly bifurcated into countries above 15% (Cambodia, Thailand, and Viet Nam) and below 15% (Indonesia, Lao PDR, Malaysia, Myanmar, and the Philippines[4]). Unique average growth rates of top performing ADB member countries in each category were applied (1.8% average growth for countries with a ratio greater than 15% and 2.44% average growth for countries with ratios below 15% over the 5-year period).

---

[2] World Bank. 2020. *Data—Tax-to-GDP Ratio*. https://data.worldbank.org/indicator/GC.TAX.TOTL.GD.ZS.

[3] Ratios in 2020 assumed to be the same as in the latest available year of data based on World Bank data—typically 2018 or 2019.

[4] World Bank data classifies Thailand's tax-to-GDP ratio in 2018 as below 15% (14.9%), but ADB data classifies it above 15% (16.4%). To maintain consistency with the data used for other countries in this analysis, World Bank data were used. Other Southeast Asian countries with minor data differences between the two databases are unaffected in this analysis as their classifications remain the same.

- **Step 3—Calculation of cumulative upside against business-as-usual.** Under the business-as-usual (BAU) projections over 2020–2025, tax-to-GDP ratios were assumed to remain constant as in the latest year of available data. The cumulative upside was calculated by totaling the incremental difference in tax revenue between the BAU and forecast scenarios for each year for each country.

▶ **Bottom-up methodology—Sizing Individual Opportunities to Expand Tax Revenue**

This exercise provides an indication of the strongest individual opportunities to expand tax revenues for five focus countries—Cambodia, Indonesia, Myanmar, the Philippines, and Thailand. Of the 10 opportunities described in Section III, six were sized. Under the category of "expanding the tax base," all five opportunities were sized—increasing PIT progressivity, taxing wealth, taxing property, environmental taxation, and taxing digital services. Under "enhancing tax compliance," one opportunity was sized—curbing VAT fraud; reducing informality was not sized as this has overlapped with curbing VAT fraud and itself consists of a broader set of levers to reduce the size of the shadow economy. The three opportunities under the category of "improving tax administration" were not sized as projections and case studies of improvements in these areas at the aggregate level are largely unavailable.

The methodology used in each of the opportunities is described below:

- **Increasing personal income tax progressivity.** The potential increase in PIT revenues from better progressivity was sized, in terms of an increase in tax revenues calculated as a share of 2019 GDP. It is assumed that countries can gain 0.3% of GDP in additional tax revenues, in line with projections of the International Monetary Fund (IMF) for Indonesia from deploying this lever.[5] This approach provides a useful indicator of the potential tax increase from improving the progressivity of PIT but has some key limitations. First, the study is specific to Indonesia's PIT structure, which has a limited incidence on the middle class— other countries have different structures that may be more progressive. Second, specific tax rates would impact consumption differently in other countries.

- **Taxing wealth.** The potential increase in tax revenues through the introduction of a wealth tax was sized, and the increase is calculated as a share of 2019 GDP. It is assumed that countries can gain 0.3% of GDP in additional tax revenues, in line with IMF analysis on Iceland on the impact of a 1.5% wealth tax on net capital.[6] This wealth tax was applied on assets above a certain threshold which qualified the top 2.2% of income earners as required to pay the tax. This approach similarly provides a useful but simplified indicator of potential tax gains from wealth taxes—the impact of wealth taxes across countries is contingent on the current distribution of income and wealth and the specific tax rates applied.

- **Taxing property.** The potential increase in tax revenues through an increase in property taxes was sized, and the increase is calculated as a share of 2019 GDP. It is assumed that property tax collections in each of the five focus countries match the Organisation for Economic Co-operation and Development (OECD) average of 1.9% of GDP, up from their current levels (Cambodia, 0.6%; Indonesia, 0.2%; Philippines, 0.5%; and Thailand, 0.5%).[7] Matching the OECD average is a useful target, but the impact of property taxes in countries is similarly contingent on the structure of property markets, current levels of ownership, expectations of property value movement, and other factors.

---

5   IMF. 2019. *Indonesia: Selected Issues.* IMF Country Report No. 19/251. https://www.imf.org/~/media/Files/Publications/ CR/2019/1IDNEA2019002.ashx.

6   IMF. 2010. *Iceland: Improving the Equity and Revenue Productivity of the Icelandic Tax System.* http://www.imf.org/external/pubs/ft/scr/2010/ cr10213.pdf.

7   ADB. 2020. *A Comparative Analysis of Tax Administration in Asia and the Pacific.* 2020 Edition. https://www.adb.org/sites/default/files/ publication/569626/tax-administration-asia-pacific-2020.pdf.

- **Environmental taxation.** The potential increase in environmentally related tax revenues through an increase in these taxes was sized, and the increase was calculated as a share of 2019 GDP. It is assumed that environmental tax collections in each of the five focus countries match the OECD average of 1.54% of GDP, up from their current levels (the Philippines, 0.38%; Thailand, 0%; remaining countries assumed to match the Association of Southeast Asian Nations average of 0.21%).[8] Matching the OECD average is again a useful target, but current levels and future impact of environmental taxes vary significantly between countries based on the energy mix, expected future developments in renewable energy, current excise taxes and subsidies on energy, permits and cap-and-trade systems, the state of carbon markets, and other factors.

- **Taxing digital services.** The potential increase in tax revenues through an introduction or increase in taxes on digital goods and services as well as additional turnover taxes on company profits to reduce base erosion and profit shifting was sized, and the increase was calculated as an increase in 2019 corporate taxes. An analysis by the OECD estimates that globally, between 4% and 10% of corporate tax revenues are lost from base erosion and profit shifting practices annually.[9] It is assumed that the focus countries can increase their tax revenues through this opportunity by the equivalent of an additional 4% of corporate tax collections in 2019. This is a useful illustration of the impact of this lever, but countries stand to gain differently than a standardized increase as the size of their digital economy and current digital tax regimes vary. For instance, Indonesia has already implemented a digital goods and service tax, which has already led to $21 million in collections in its first 3 months of operation in 2020.[10]

- **Curbing value-added tax fraud.** The potential increase in VAT revenues through increased transaction reporting through digital means, calculated as an increase in VAT collections. It is assumed that countries can secure 8% additional VAT revenues through such interventions, in line with an analysis from Belgium that reported 8% higher VAT revenues annually from installing electronic cash registers with transaction monitoring and reporting to local tax authorities.[11] The success of such measures is dependent on the scale of rollout and the ability of tax authorities to process transaction data and identify fraud. Reducing VAT fraud through monitoring is also only one option to increase VAT revenues—others include reducing overall VAT rates to disincentivize VAT fraud altogether. Countries, therefore, stand to benefit differently from the application of different levers.

---

[8]   OECD. 2020. *Environmental Taxation.* https://www.oecd.org/environment/environmentaltaxation.htm.

[9]   OECD. 2020. *OECD Presents Analysis Showing Significant Impact of Proposed International Tax Reforms.* https://www.oecd.org/tax/beps/oecd-presents-analysis-showing-significant-impact-of-proposed-international-tax-reforms.htm.

[10] *The Jakarta Post.* 2020. Indonesia Collects $209m in Digital Tax as of October. https://www.thejakartapost.com/news/2020/11/24/indonesia-collects-20-9m-in-digital-tax-as-of-october.html.

[11] OECD. 2016. *Technologies for Better Tax Administration: A Practical Guide for Revenue Bodies.* Paris: OECD Publishing. https://read.oecd-ilibrary.org/taxation/technologies-for-better-tax-administration_9789264256439-en#page1.

CPSIA information can be obtained
at www.ICGtesting.com
Printed in the USA
BVHW022232200722
642674BV00013B/110

9 789292 695057